KT-489-849

IT'S A BIT OF A MOUTHFUL

To DAVID
I WISH YOU WELL
REGARDS

Geoff

IT'S A BIT OF A MOUTHFUL

Into and Out of the Mouths of Babes, and Sucklings

GEOFF GRAHAM
Author of
How to Become the Parent You Never Had

REAL OPTIONS PRESS

First published in Great Britain 1987 by
Real Options Press
Dunsopp House
Lucy Street
Blaydon upon Tyne.
NE21 5PU

© Geoff Graham 1987
All rights reserved No part of this book may be reproduced or transmitted in any form or by any means whatsoever without prior written permission from the publisher except in the case of brief quotations embodied in critical articles and reviews.

BRITISH LIBRARY CATALOGUING IN PUBLICATION DATA

Graham Geoff
It's a Bit of a Mouthful;
Into and out of the mouths of babes and sucklings
1. Psychotherapy
1. Title
616.89'14   RC480

ISBN 0 9511951 1 5

Printed by Martin's of Berwick. Sea View Works Spittal, Berwick upon Tweed. TD15 1RS.

Contents

Page

Introduction   1

PART 1: Oral Gratification—using the mouth as a defence.

Chapter 1.
   Obesity. Why do we over-eat and what can we do
   about it? Why do so many diets fail?   11

Chapter 2.
   Smoking. How do we stop?   26

Chapter 3.
   Alcoholism. Can we stop drinking to excess?   37

Chapter 4.
   Oral Sex.   49

Chapter 5.
   Anorexia Nervosa. The slimmers' disease and
   related disorders.   59

Chapter 6.
   Verbal Diarrhoea. The constant talker.   80

Chapter 7.
   Nail biting and Thumb sucking. How to stop.   86

Chapter 8.
   Grinding your teeth away, and allied behaviour.   94

PART 2: Defending our mouth to the point where the defence becomes the problem—Why do we do it? Can we stop?

Chapter 9.
   The Dental Phobic.   109

Chapter 10
   Dentures. Why do some people reject them even
   when they have no teeth?   124

Chapter. 11
   Conclusions.   135

Appendix.
   The Exercises   142

The Author

Geoff Graham started using hypnosis in dentistry in 1960. He formed the Northern Counties Branch of The British Society of Medical and Dental Hypnosis in 1969. Since this time he has been involved in lecturing and running courses and workshops both in this country and Europe, North and South America, Australia, and the Far East. In 1972 he was made a Foreign Fellow of the American Society of Clinical Hypnosis. In 1973 while attending The Pan American Congress of Hypnosis in Brazil he was made a Member of Honour at that Conference. In 1974 he was made an Honorary Fellow of the Singapore Society of Clinical Hypnosis. He is a Founder Fellow of the British Society of Medical and Dental Hypnosis and has acted as a National Assessor for the Certificate of Accreditation issued by that society and possesses a Certificate in his own right.

He has spent over a year attending part-time training as a Primal Therapist with the International Society of Primal Therapists organized by Dr. W. Swartley. Although he is not a hospital consultant both B.U.P.A. and P.P.P. accept Geoff Graham on a consultant basis when patients are referred to him by other Hospital Consultants. He has now treated well over two thousand patients with hypnosis, most of whom have been referred to him. He is also a member of the International Society of Hypnosis.

He feels many patients seeking help with psychological problems get very little real help, and has written this book to make the information and experience he has had the privilege to obtain from patients, available both to therapists, but more importantly to the intelligent public so that they may be in a position to help themselves, with the carefully structured self-help exercises outlined in this book.

Acknowledgments

I would like once again to offer my sincere thanks to all those who have helped me produce this book, especially to Elizabeth who was responsible for the first, and subsequent editings. Also thanks are due to Michael and Peter who read through the manuscript and gave most valuable advice, on both the content, and presentation. I would also like to thank Brian who taught me to use a computer and word processor. It can spell better than I can. Mostly, I would like to thank and dedicate this book to my patients, who have taught me more than anyone, both with the theory and the treatment outlined in this book. Without them there would be no book.

Introduction

'Once upon a time' most of us were very comfortable, safe, secure, needed, necessary, wanted and loved. Our every need was supplied immediately, without us having to ask for anything. At that time we were very tiny, safe and warm in an enclosed secure cave. In the background there was the comforting rhythmical beat supplying us with all our needs. Then one day nature dealt us a dastardly blow, the walls of our cave began to contract. We were slowly pushed and shoved down the entrance of our cave, out into the light.

For many of us this first journey was very frightening and painful, made all the more so because it was unknown, and probably most of the difficulties were quite unexpected. Then all of a sudden we were out in the light and for the first time in our lives we were completely on our own, and we became 'I' [see fig. 1. below] Our life-line, which had supplied our every need, was cut, our skins began to dry and the air began to tingle and in most cases the temperature was much cooler. Our ears began to hear unmuffled sounds that were often much louder than we had been used to. Our lungs opened and we had to breathe air for the first time, and we perhaps smelled and tasted things for the first time. Although our eyes may not yet have opened, we were aware of the brightness around us. The rhythmical beat that had comforted and provided everything for the first nine months of our life, was nowhere to be found. (If a tape recording of a beating heart is played softly and slowly to new born babies many of them will go to sleep, and if those heart beats are played louder and quicker the baby will wake up. This is providing that the baby is neurologically normal, and it is one method of testing new born babies to see if they are normal.)

Senses

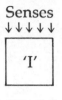

[Fig.1.]

Our minds, which had no concepts at that stage of being 'Out,' were continually being bombarded by stimuli from our five senses, of which we knew nothing, nor even how to cope with them. In order to escape this bombardment most of us went to sleep and shut off our consciousness, until such times as we could begin to understand these stimuli, little by little. To do this we began to build in our minds a set of concepts that helped us to understand what things, and the stimuli, meant. It was rather like building a reference library that would help us to cope with the unknown, or making a new computer program for the bio-computer we call our brain. Each concept we learned was another book in our mental library, a new program. There were a number of books already in that library from conception, inter-uterine life and, of course, birth itself. [See my first book **How to be The Parent You Never Had.**]

Most people throughout their lives experience fear of the unknown and try to help themselves by building more and more concepts, or putting more and more books in their mental library to cope with the fear. For example, many children will fear having their hair cut for the first time. Most of them will fear their first day at school—this is often a combination of fear of the unknown, coupled with yet another separation from mother. Many adults fear a new exam, or interview—fear of the unknown. So we just build more and more concepts [or programs] in our mind to help us cope with this unknown. If we again think of these concepts in terms of a reference library, perhaps one of the first books we put in that library after we get 'out' is a about being aware of our tummy being empty. We notice we are uncomfortable and may even hurt, so we draw air into our lungs and then push it out forcibly, at the same time we do

something in our throats and the resultant noise makes
someone put something in our mouth. Then we suck on
whatever is put in our mouth and a warm soothing liquid
goes down our throats and we are comforted. The pain goes,
and at the same time hopefully a close contact is again
experienced with mother. When our tummy is full we go to
sleep once again to escape from the unknown.

There are various needs to be satisfied, so we add new
books to our library. These needs can be divided into social
and selfish needs. *[see fig. 2. and 3. below]* The first is the basic
need to survive, Then we all need love, from the moment of
conception until the day we die, so we make books about
how we can get love and what that means, especially if we
have suffered any 'wipe-out' during the birth. [See my book
How to Become The Parent You Never Had.] Love is to have
one's needs satisfied without having to ask for anything.
This comes from the womb, but is often wiped out at birth.

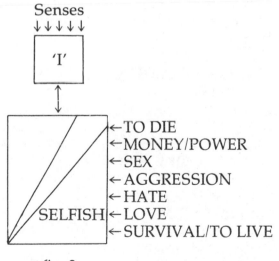

fig. 2.

Then we need a concept to defend against not getting love.
That concept is hate. Hate is not opposite to love, but a
defence against not getting love. It evolves from 'I love you,
why don't you love me. I hate you for not loving me. There

must be something wrong with me. I must be hateful.' We need a way of expressing that hate, in aggression. Then we need a way of expressing love, in sex. Then we seek security, in power and money or possessions, especially if we lost the feeling of security at birth . But these attempts to find security fail because security is a gut feeling of being loved which once again we get from that cosmic consciousness in the womb. I often get challenged about the desire to die, but I remind you of Holmes and Rahé and their work on the stress of adjusting to change. We get ill if we are subjected to too much stress, because we want 'out of this world' when things get too tough. [See **How to be The Parent You Never Had**].

The above are all selfish needs but we soon learn that we can't always have what we want, especially, when we want it. We have to develop another side to our library, to cope with our social needs. *[See fig. 3. below].*

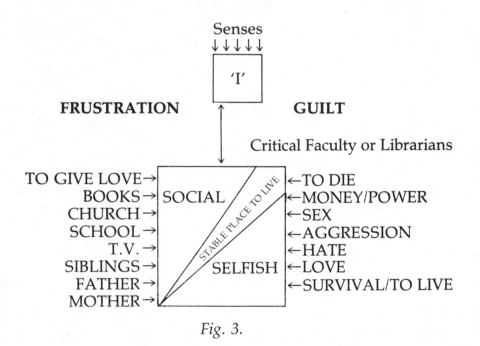

Fig. 3.

On the social side, mother is far and away the first one to influence us and poor old father comes a very poor second.

So women who want 'equality' want a retrograde step because they are superior, and always have been from the birth of their first child. Then come brothers and sisters, adding more concepts about them and yourself, and how you feel about them. Then comes the curse of the present day, the T.V. Children become 'square-eyed' from watching T.V. at a very early age these days. Then we have to make concepts about school, religion, books on how to give love. We soon learn that the best way to receive love is to give love. If we can both give and receive love we are rarely unhappy neurotics, and we can cuddle both our parents affectionately, or we have become our own parent and don't need our real parents. [See my book **How to Become The Parent You Never Had.**]

Perception is strictly controlled by our learned concepts and if any of those concepts are wrong, or no longer relevant, then our perception is wrong and no longer relevant. That is until we put a new book in the library and start to perceive by the new concept. Many of the concepts were formed when we were hurting or suffering great, unfulfilled need. In those cases the concepts are most often wrong, but because of the hurt attached to them, we often do not dare change them for fear of feeling the hurt. In these cases our perception is wrong and we seem to have little ability to change, or have any options in the connected behaviour.

To demonstrate the point of perception being controlled by learned concepts I would like to give you some examples. The first is a case of impotence that I was asked to treat in a man called William. William was from the Far East and he told me that in his culture it was quite normal for young boys and young men to have homosexual relationships. Therefore these relationships were quite acceptable to him, however he was now having some difficulty in getting an erection when he wanted to make love to his wife. He had been to see another hypnotist who had told him, while he was in hypnosis, that homosexuality was very wrong, and he must suppress all thoughts of that behaviour. He was told that if he succeeded in doing this, his relationship with his wife would improve, because he would no longer feel guilty about his homosexual thoughts. He was not aware he felt guilty about his homosexual thoughts. This treatment had had a very temporary improvement in his potency but after a very brief improvement he was now getting much worse.

I asked him if it was acceptable for fathers to have a sexual relationship with their sons, and on being told a very definite 'no', I asked him if fathers and sons ever cuddled, and again the answer was a very firm 'no'. And so we perhaps see why a certain culture brings about the need for homosexuality. If fathers don't cuddle and hold their sons then the sons will most likely search symbolically for that love in other males. After explaining this he felt much better about his homosexual thoughts. Then, after a little more questioning, I found out that his wife had been unfaithful with another man, and it was William's fear that he wouldn't be as good as the other man that made William impotent. He still loved his wife and wanted her, so we worked on that, making him much more aware of his love for her, than his fear about the other man. Fairly soon his potency returned and his fear disappeared.

Another example of how learned concepts affect our perception occurred in a true story reported in the press in the spring of 1974, and I am sure there have been other similar reports like this one. A Japanese soldier was discovered hiding on a remote Pacific island ever since the second world war between America and Japan. He was not aware that the war was over and he knew nothing of any of the other developments that had occurred in the meantime. He found it was impossible to live in the world as he found it, as his concept of the world, and of surrender, were completely outdated. As he couldn't change his concepts, his only way out was to commit suicide, which he did. This shows the extent that people will go to if they cannot change learned concepts.

An artist friend of mine gives a lecture to his students on perception. To demonstrate a point, he shows a slide of his small son looking through a reeded glass door. On asking the students what they see on that slide, they all report 'a small boy looking through a glass door'. None of them report a six-eyed monster with three mouths and three noses, and yet that is what appears on the slide because of the reeded glass. Because they all have a concept of reeded glass and a little boy, that's what they see. It would be much too uncomfortable for them to see a monster, and yet if they were beings from another planet with no concept of reeded glass or little boys, they would see the monster. I hope these examples show you how learned concepts affect perception, and the extent to which people will go because of that perception.

In order to sort out these concepts, or 'reference books', we employ our critical faculty, or 'librarians'. While we are in the state we call hypnosis, we can often give the librarians of the mind the day off, when we can then go into the library and read the books for ourselves, and put new ones into our reference library so that our perception is altered. Without doing that, if our concepts are wrong, our perception is wrong and we can't change.

If we live using only the selfish side of our library we suffer from guilt. If on the other hand we live using only the social side of our library we feel frustrated. At first, fresh out of the womb, we are entirely selfish, but then as we grow older and take on more responsibility we have to become more social. The only stable place to live is somewhere between the two, tending to become more social as we grow older.

In Part 1 of this book I have taken certain behaviours in which we use our mouths as a defence, and tried to show how the concepts are formed, and how they affect behaviour, and what we can do to change that behaviour when it is no longer desirable. In Part 2, I have tried to show why the mouth is so important to us, and why sometimes we over-defend it, to the extent, of that defence becoming a problem.

Geoff Graham. August 1986.

PART 1

Oral Gratification—
using the mouth as a defence

CHAPTER 1

Obesity. Why do we over-eat and what can we do about it? Why do so many diets fail?

There are as many reasons for over eating as there are fat people. The standard treatment for obesity is a diet. More drastic treatment is to wire the jaws together so that people can't eat, or even surgically remove some of the gut so that food absorption is reduced. All these treatments are directed at the symptom of being fat. None of them are directed at why we over-eat. Perhaps that is why so many people fail in either losing weight in the first place, or maintaining the healthy weight obtained by dieting. I would go so far as to say that some seventy-five percent of fat people fail in their quest to be slim. Many of them seem to end up even fatter after their unsuccessful attempt at slimming.

We blame our hormones, or our metabolic rate, or brown fat cells. All these excuses are playing the 'blame game'. It is we who are over-eating. Fat people are fat because they eat more than their body needs to maintain a healthy weight and the excess calories are deposited round the body in brown fat cells. Treatment of obesity should be directed at why we need to over-eat, but it rarely is, and that's why so many people fail to be slim. Most people treating obesity do nothing about the dynamic process of why we over-eat, consequently when we stop dieting we have the devil's own job not to over-eat again.

So why do we over-eat? and what can we do about it? There has to be a reason for everything we do, and those

11

reasons are concepts stored in our mind like the reference books in the library mentioned in the introduction. How, and when did we write those books? and why do we follow those concepts blindly when we want to be thin?

One of the first books put in our library after birth is about survival. We eat to survive. At the same time by eating we get close contact with mother, as well as reducing tension and making us more comfortable, and reducing stress. If we have to cry for some time, before anyone puts something in our mouth which we suck on to get food, we become pretty uptight and distressed. When we suck and get food that distress is relieved. So already in the first few hours of being 'out' in the world we have made some important concepts about eating. Eating is necessary to survive, makes us less lonely by bringing us into closer contact, reduces tension and stress and makes us more comfortable.

When we have finished eating our tummy is full, so eating fills an emptiness, and we can go to sleep comfortably. So in the first few hours after birth we have put six books that tell us about eating, in our mental library. Is it any wonder that there are a lot of fat people? All of the above concepts are reinforced, over and over, every day. If we choose to eat as a defence against loneliness, stress, tension or because we feel empty for some other reason than lack of food; because of those learned concepts, then that defence is reinforced, especially if we eat without being hungry to solve one of the other things. If this defence is used over and over again, pretty soon we don't know why we are eating, and if it is not because we are hungry we learn not to feel full, so we can eat more. This is just another book that will defeat our efforts at dieting.

When we are small and growing our parents tell us to eat all our food so that we will grow big and strong. Many parents praise their children for eating all their food like a good boy or good girl. It is sometimes the only praise the parents give. Children are reminded about the starving children of the world and told not to leave any food that those less fortunate children would love to have now. What a stupid way to make children eat: even if the child doesn't eat the food the starving children aren't going to get it. This is just another way of making a book about guilt if you leave anything on your plate. Some parents reward their children with sweets when they have been good. So now we have a whole new set of concepts, or books about eating, in our library. Eating makes us strong, we are very good to eat everything on our plate. We won't need feel guilty if we eat everything. Eating is a reward for being good so if I want to reward myself I must eat sweets. We all accept that eating is a reward and over-eating is a 'better' reward—consider the big blow-out celebration meals we have at birthdays, anniversaries, graduations or any other event of which we are proud!

When there is more than one child in the family, parents often hold the one who eats the most, as an example to the others of how good the big eater is. The one who eats the most is the best. This is generally done by parents who are overweight themselves and can't recognise greed, if they did they would feel greedy themselves. Just another book in the library—to be the best eat the most, or even to win eat the most, even if you can't win in any other way. Children of fat parents often want to be like their parents, especially if they admire their parents for something. That something that they admire in their parents may well have nothing to do with over-eating, but unconsciously the child will over-eat to be like its parent.

If mother over-eats when she is carrying her baby it is possible that the baby makes a book about a high blood sugar level being normal, even before it gets 'out'. Consequently, if the blood sugar level drops to normal when it is out it may well feel hungry and eat to raise the level to be the same as mother's. There seems to be a link with the incidence of diabetes in people whose parents have diabetes.

I hope you are now beginning to see the truth in my statement at the beginning of this chapter that there are as many reasons for over-eating as there are fat people. When you remember that perception is governed by learned concepts, it's a wonder any of us are thin.

So why aren't we all fat? Remember in the introduction I

said that if concepts were wrong then perception is wrong until we put a new book in the library and start to perceive by the new, and hopefully more accurate concept. If, however, the old concept is made when we are hurting, we are reluctant to change the concept for fear of feeling the hurt. Whether or not we change it depends upon how much pain there is attached to the concept, upon how many times it has been reinforced, and how much other unresolved pain we have in our system. Any other unresolved pain may well threaten to attach itself to a release of pain, making any attempt at release too frightening.

If we just stop people from eating, without doing anything about the faulty concept that makes them over-eat in the first place, most of our attempts will be doomed to failure. I once read some case histories in a hypnosis journal where all the patients failed to lose weight because the hypnotist had failed to recognise these dynamic factors behind over-eating. The hypnotist, quite incorrectly, concluded that hypnosis is of little use in cases of obesity. The hypnotist was at fault, not hypnosis. She hadn't used any techniques to alter the patients' learned concepts, consequently no weight loss was achieved.

So already we may have twelve books in our library which, if not changed, will make us over-eat

1. We must eat to survive and grow.
2. We must eat not to be lonely and if we are lonely we must eat.
3. We must eat to reduce stress
4. We must eat to reduce tension.
5. Eating makes us feel less empty inside.
6. If we have used eating to relieve any of the above, then we have probably learned not to feel full when we eat, so that we can go on eating more, to go on relieving any of the above.
7. Eat everything on my plate or I will feel guilty, so I eat even when I'm not hungry, or even when I feel guilty about anything, to relieve the guilt.

8. Eat to win and be good. If I feel bad I must eat and I won't feel bad any more.

9. Eating is a reward, so eat when I feel a need to reward myself, especially eat sweet things.

10. Eating makes me strong, or warm, so if I feel weak or cold, eat a lot.

11. I respect Mother or Father and they are fat and I would like to be like them, so eat to be like them.

12. Mother's high blood sugar level is normal for me, so I feel hungry when mine drops to normal.

13. There can always be other concepts making us over-eat.

Any or all of the above concepts may be dynamic forces in our unconscious mind, making us over-eat. If you are going to help someone to get slim it is far better to find out which of the above factors are making them over eat, and help the patient to write new books about any, or all, of their immature and faulty concepts, while they are dieting. This is especially necessary after they have reached their target weight, otherwise they may well just over-eat again.

People who are trying to lose weight and are not succeeding are eating more than they need to lose weight. They do that either by having too high an intake in their diet, or by cheating. If their diet is too much, just reduce the intake but it is much more common for them to be cheating. How do people cheat and why do they when they want to be thin? First of all, they cheat because one or more of the above twelve reasons are making them eat more than they need. Perhaps there's even another reason, and that's why I have put thirteen in the list above.

How do people cheat? First of all there's the secret eater. The one who raids the fridge or pantry late at night, when everybody has gone to bed; who buys food and eats it before they get home, throwing away any packaging, to leave no trace of their illicit eating. The one who quickly rams food down their throat when they think no one is looking. They seem to think if no-one sees them eat they can deny having had the food, when everyone can see they are eating too much because they are well over weight and not losing any.

Who do they think they are kidding?

Then there's the one who denies they have had many calories at any previous meal so they can eat a little more at the present one. They still stay overweight but deny they are eating very much. Then there is the one who says they hate the taste of whatever diet they are on, just to defeat the diet, and justify eating something else as well as the diet. Another way of cheating is to feel weak, so they will have to eat more to keep up their strength, or complain of the cold and have to eat to keep warm. Again there are a thousand ways of cheating on a diet and the people who fail to lose weight know all about those ways. It is plain to see they cheat because they never get any thinner and yet they deny cheating and expect people to believe them.

Yet another way they cheat is to lie about their weight. The only way to defeat this method of cheating is to weigh them yourself each time they attend for therapy.

So how are we to help someone to diet and get slim and stay slim?

The Treatment of Obesity.

At the beginning it is necessary to ask pertinent questions to establish if any of the concepts discussed above are present causing the patient to over-eat. This can be first done in the waking state watching the patient very carefully for any give away signs of deceit.

You can start off with 'When you were a little girl ,or boy, did your parents encourage you to eat everything on your plate? If yes, did they praise you when you finished everything? If you left anything did they remind you of the starving people in the world and make you feel guilty? When you were good did they reward you with some sweets? When did you first start to put on excess weight? What was happening to you at that time? Were there any difficulties at the time you first put weight on, like changing school, or taking exams, or anything that was stressful. *[Did you first learn to eat to overcome stress]* Were either of your parents overweight? Was your mother overweight when she was carrying you? Do you, or did you, particularly admire either of your parents, especially the overweight one? Can you cuddle both of your parents affectionately? (See importance of this question in **'How to become the Parent You Never Had').**

'Do you recognise any factors in the present that make you eat? Do you eat when you feel stressful? Do you eat when you feel lonely? Do you often feel guilty? Do you ever feel your life is empty? Do you eat when you are angry? Do you eat when you are bored? Do you ever lie about your weight? Do you sometimes cheat by not telling anyone what you have just eaten? Do you sometimes eat secretly? Do you eat quickly and finish before most people?'

After this questioning in the waking state it is useful to do some questioning in the hypnotic state using 'Ideo-Motor Finger Questioning' So the first exercise in this book is to find a way to enter the hypnotic state quickly and easily.

EXERCISE 1.
Find a comfortable chair preferably with a high back which will support your head. Sit comfortably in the chair and rest your head on the back. Place your feet with your soles flat on the ground. At this point I always suggest that female patients remove their shoes. Ladies tend to take off their shoes when returning home after work, a shopping expedition, an evening out etc. and it is therefore a major aid to their relaxation. Place both your arms comfortably and lightly on each armrest of the chair; if there are no armrests on the chair, place one hand upon each knee. Do not fold your arms or clasp your hands, as both these behaviours are defensive. Look straight ahead of you, then, without altering the position of your head, turn your eyes up to look up towards your eyebrows. Turn them up as high as you can without moving your head. Keeping your eyes turned up close your eyes. (SPIEGEL'S EYEROLL INDUCTION)

Now relax your eyes, let them become so relaxed, so heavy they feel they just won't open, and hang on to that feeling. Now let that feeling spread through the whole of your body. Let your body sink comfortably down into the chair. (ELMAN DEEPENING)

While your body is sinking down into the chair turn your mind inward to look at your mind (GEOFF GRAHAM & N.L.P) Let your mind feel as if it can float. (SPIEGEL)
End of exercise One. This exercise also appears in 'How to Become the Parent You Never Had'.

The next exercise also appears in the above book and that exercise is to set up an ideo-motor finger response.

EXERCISE 2.   IDEO-MOTOR FINGER RESPONSES.

When you are talking to someone in a perfectly normal state of consciousness, and you are asking them a question to which they answer 'yes', watch their head. Ask them another question to which they will answer 'yes' and watch their head again. Most people answering 'yes' to a question will not only say 'yes', but at the same time they will nod their head. Ask them without telling them, 'what did they do when they answered the question' and most of them won't have a clue what they did, showing that the nod of the head is an unconscious answer. The same is true of a negative answer when they shake the head.

While people are talking, even in a normal state of consciousness, two parts of their mind are listening, paying attention and answering. The conscious mind is answering by verbally saying 'yes' or 'no', but at the same time the unconscious mind is also answering by nodding or shaking the head. This nodding or shaking of the head is called an ideo-motor response. It is a response from the unconscious mind. We often set this up deliberately so that we can explore the unconscious mind. If we are being affected by something which happened to us long ago, we must have a memory of it somewhere within us; if this were not the case, it would not be affecting us now. This memory, however, is often long since forgotten consciously, but it is still in the unconscious somewhere. We can explore the unconscious mind in an altered state by asking the unconscious to answer our questions by lifting a finger of one of our hands, say the index finger of the left hand, or often it is better to let the unconscious mind choose which finger it will use. It can use one finger for 'yes' and another for 'no', in this way we can ask it 'yes or no' questions. You can even have an 'I don't know' finger, and an 'I don't want to answer' finger, but I feel having too many alternatives often confuses the answer. We are much less used to lying with our finger so we may well get a more honest answer this way. It is not, however, infallible and the finger can lie. So we just ask our unconscious mind if it will answer in this way and if it will, will it please lift a 'yes' finger. One finger should rise. Establish a 'no' finger in the same way and if you get a response both times you should be able to ask it some more questions that may help you to have more options. It it not so easy to do this by yourself but if it is first done with a therapist many patients can do it by themselves. The skill is often in knowing what to ask it, and what to do about it when you get an answer.

Having now set up an ideo-motor finger response you explain to the patient in the hypnotic state the facts about learned concepts and then you ask the patients unconscious mind if it will answer questions about any learned concepts which are still active regarding over-eating. If it will answer would it please lift the 'Yes' finger. When the finger lifts, indicating its willingness to respond ask 'is there a concept in your unconscious mind about having to eat to grow and survive?' 'If there is, the 'yes' finger will rise, if no the 'no' finger will rise'. Make a note of the answer. Go through all thirteen books in the mental library shown above on pages 14 & 15. For number thirteen, ask is there any other concept in your unconscious mind that makes you over-eat? Make a note of all the answers. For each positive answer it is necessary to reframe the concept to a more suitable way of helping the patient to deal with his or her problem without over-eating. The way to do that is shown in the exercises below.

EXERCISE 3.
If there is a positive answer to No.1 contact the part of your mind that is helping you to grow, and thank it for helping you to grow when you were small. When that part of your mind is listening, paying attention and wanting to help, and

is willing to negotiate, let it lift your 'Yes' finger. When your finger lifts, remind the part that you have finished growing upwards and the only way you can grow now is outwards, and you don't want to do that.

Would the part of your mind that is helping you to grow please now help you to maintain a healthy weight without growing any more. If it will, let it lift your 'Yes' finger. When the finger rises thank it for agreeing to help you in this new way.

EXERCISE 4.
If there is a positive answer to No.2 and your mind is helping you to cope with loneliness by making you eat to feel less alone, thank it for trying to help you. Ask the part of your mind that is making you eat when you feel lonely, when it is listening, paying attention, wanting to help, and is willing to negotiate, to lift your 'Yes' finger. When the finger lifts, respectfully remind the mind that you would be able to make more friends and be much more confident in meeting new people when you are less fat. Ask it to help you to get, and stay, more slim, so that you will be confident to go out and meet more friends to be less lonely. When that part agrees to help you in this new way let it lift your 'Yes' finger. When the finger lifts, thank it.

EXERCISE 5.
If your mind is helping you to reduce stress by eating as in No.3, or tension as in No.4 contact that part of your mind, and when it is listening, paying attention, wanting to help, and is willing to negotiate, let it lift your 'Yes' finger. Thank it for trying to help you to cope with stress or tension but respectfully remind it that by making you fat it is now increasing your stress/tension and the way it is trying to help you has become a problem. There are many more efficient ways of reducing stress/tension now that you are older. [See my first book **How to Become the Parent You Never Had,** chapter 6. pages 68-74.]

Ask the part of your mind that is making you eat to reduce stress/tension to help you in four or five of the alternative ways, as outlined in my first book, instead of making you over-eat. When it is willing to do that, have it indicate its willingness by lifting your 'Yes' finger. When the finger lifts, thank it.

EXERCISE 6.
If you are experiencing an empty feeling in life and your mind is trying to help you cope with that feeling by making you over-eat in an attempt to fill that emptiness, respectfully remind the mind that the empty feeling has nothing to do with your tummy being empty. To fill your tummy to the point of making you fat will most probably make you end up even more empty because you will become ashamed of your size and stop going out. When that part is listening, paying attention, wanting to help, and is willing to negotiate, let it lift your 'Yes' finger. When the finger lifts, thank it for trying to help but respectfully remind it that the way it is helping you has now become a problem. You would be much more able to fill that empty feeling in life, if you were smart and fit and not over-weight. So ask it if it would help you to cope with that feeling by helping you to reduce your intake of food so that you become smarter, more fit, and a normal weight. Thank it when it agrees.

EXERCISE 7.
If you get a positive answer to question 6 and you don't have an efficient switch off feeling to eating when you have had a reasonable sized meal, respectfully remind the part of your mind that it is trying to help you cope with any of the problems above by making it easy to eat more without feeling full. Ask it to change by letting you become aware of the amount of food you have eaten at any meal. Respectfully remind it that over eating has now become a problem and you would rather not eat so much. Ask it to help you to stop over eating from now.

EXERCISE 8.
If you regularly eat everything on your plate just because it's there, and you have been taught to clean your plate or feel

guilty you need to relearn that behaviour. The best way to do that is to tell your mind that it is much better, and healthier for you to throw away any unwanted food than eat it and become fat. To remind you of this, always leave at least one mouthful on your plate and throw it away, telling yourself that you don't want it, until you can do that easily, and without any feelings of guilt. When you have no guilt feeling as a reaction to throwing away food, ask your mind to continue to help you to only eat that which you want.

EXERCISE 9.
If you are eating to win, or to feel that you are a good person, find the part of your mind that is making you do this and respectfully remind it that now that you have become over-weight you can feel much better if you don't over-eat, and will win when you reach your target weight.

EXERCISE 10.
If you have learned to reward yourself with sweets, or food, remind your mind that now you have a weight problem the reward will be getting slimmer. You will feel much healthier when you have lost some weight and that will be a reward in itself.

EXERCISE 11.
If you are eating because you feel weak, or cold, tell your mind that a good balanced diet will make you a lot stronger when you are not having to carry all that excess weight about, and you can easily put more clothes on if you feel cold.

EXERCISE 12.
If you respect something in your mother or father you can be like them without being fat like them. Tell your mind while in a hypnotic state that you can be even better than either of your parent by being like them, but without their handicap of being over-weight.

EXERCISE 13.
If you feel hungry all the time, unless you are eating, tell your

mind in a hypnotic state that you would really like to only feel hungry when your blood sugar is getting low.

If there are other concepts making you over-eat then reframe those concepts as in the above exercises. If you get a 'No' answer to all the thirteen questions on pages 14 & 15, and you are not losing weight, your ideo-motor finger is lying, otherwise you would have no difficulty in dieting and being a normal weight. If it needs to lie there must be a very strong reason for over-eating and that reason will need to be analysed before weight loss will be easy.

All the above exercises are intended to help you to not over-eat, and are essential if you want to keep your weight down when you have reached your target, and will also assist in losing weight. If a weight gain is achieved you must ask all the ideo-motor questions again and reframe any with a positive answer over again. If, however, you want to lose weight you must eat less than you need, and use up some of your body fat in order to reduce weight. The following exercises are intended to help you do that when you choose a reducing diet.

EXERCISE 14.
In a hypnotic state tell yourself to eat slowly and enjoy every mouthful so that you need fewer mouthfuls to get sufficient enjoyment.

EXERCISE 15.
'Spiegel's Split Screen'. Having done exercise 1. and reached the stage when you feel as if the mind is floating, project an image of a screen divided down the middle onto the far side of the room. If you can see the screen so much the better but if you can't just think about it. You cannot think about anything without creating an image. The image may be visual or conceptual, but either way you create an image. When you have the image of the screen, place on one side of the screen an image of yourself eating to excess and indulging in lots of fattening things. Notice in that image, yourself getting fatter and fatter in the places which you least like. On the other side of the screen have an image of yourself

eating only the diet you have chosen, and notice how you become much more the shape you wish to be. Now choose which 'You' you want to be, and tell your mind. Bring back from the screen the 'You' you want, leaving the 'You' you don't want on the other side of the room. Imagine what it would be like, enjoying being that 'You' and integrate that feeling throughout your mind. When you can feel how enjoyable it will be, being much slimmer, and sticking to an enjoyable diet, just open your eyes and be that 'You'.

Always remember if you have to do something, or want to do it, it is much easier if you find a way of enjoying doing it. Find a way of enjoying the new 'You', slimmer, healthier, and eating much less than when you were overweight. See how much more energy you will have, to do all the things you want. Notice how much more concentration you have, to do the things you want, because you are not nearly so tired as you used to be when you were so overweight. Remember when you were a stone overweight it is like carrying a stone of potatoes round with you every where you go. Notice how much more attractive you can be to the opposite sex when you are not so fat. Notice how many more options you have being normal size. See how much easier it is to get good looking clothes to fit you when you are not obese. Make sure you are going to enjoy eating the diet foods, because it is much easier to eat what you enjoy so why not programme yourself to enjoy the diet. Don't tell yourself, or anyone else, that you hate any diet food you intend to eat. You did a good job programming yourself to eat to excess so do just as good a job on dieting.

EXERCISE 16.
'Spiegel's respect for body'. When you are in a hypnotic state tell yourself that excess, or fattening foods are very bad for your body and will destroy it. Your body is your most prized and valuable possession. It is much more valuable to you than your home, or your car, or any of your jewellery, or any of your possessions. All of those things can be replaced, but your body can't. Without a body you can have none of those things. From now on, and for the rest of your life you will

give your body the respect and concern it deserves. Open your eyes and give it that respect by not over-eating.

EXERCISE 17.
In order to have an accurate body image of yourself take photographs of yourself in revealing clothes and keep looking at them until you know how you look, then tell yourself how you would like to look, when you are in a hypnotic state.

Weigh yourself at least twice a week, preferably at the same time and in the same state of dress each time. Plan on losing about three to four pounds each week until your target weight is reached. Don't try to guess your weight by the feel of your clothes. Know what a sensible weight for you should be, taking into account your build etc. Don't try on any account to go well below your target weight. Eat more if you find yourself going too low. Try and find a sensible way to keep stable at your target when you reach that level.

Do at least one of the above exercises for no more that two to three minutes every two to three hours of your waking day, until you have obtained your target, and when your target is reached do the exercises over again if ever your weight becomes unstable. If you find one exercise doesn't work then do something else.

CHAPTER 2.

Smoking. How do we stop?

Research carried out by the Office of Population Censuses and Surveys in 1984 reported in the Daily Express 4th. December 1985 that almost half of Britain's schoolchildren are hooked on smoking. Four out of ten children smoke 50 cigarettes a week on average. Playground smoking is now a £70 -£90 million pound industry. This is despite the continued fall in adult smoking. It would appear that there has been no reduction in smoking among children since 1982. While adults are giving up in increasing numbers, children are starting at eleven and even younger. Almost half are regular smokers by the time they reach the fifth form. Why do they do it? What are the books in their conceptual library? How can we try to help people to stop? The Express sent out reporters to ask the children themselves, and reported in the paper on the 5th. December 1985. 'All my mates smoke so I do it to belong.' 'I started smoking when I was twelve, I suppose I thought it made me look bigger.' 'I don't think it does much harm when you are young, although I do cough now when I get up in the morning.' 'I do it because it is an adult forbidden pleasure. I had to work at liking smoking.' The idea that it is fashionable and grown-up to smoke is holding more sway in the minds of youngsters than the fact that they may ruin their health or even die.

Even on the first day in our life when we get out of the womb we learn that to put something in our mouth and suck reduces tension and makes us closer to someone. With the breakdown in family life there seems to be an increasing need to belong to our 'mates'. It seems we will override all logical thought to belong. We can't wait to grow up so we con ourselves. Cigarette smoking is all con. Let us look at what cigarette smoking really is.

What are we doing when we smoke? We are taking dried up leaves and shredding them, and rolling them into a stick, then wrapping paper round them, putting the rolled stick in our mouth and then setting the leaves alight. We do this so that when we draw air over the burning leaves we can have burning smoke come into our mouth, and then lungs. We have to kid ourselves we like the taste. We have to work at it so that we can con ourselves that little children look grown up with a cigarette dangling out of their mouth. Who do we think we are kidding? Do we really think that a child looks anything other than a stupid youngster with a cigarette dangling out of his mouth? What happens if we rake up the leaves in the garden and burn them, and the wind whips up and blows smoke in our face? We cough and splutter and our eyes sting and run. We have to work hard to stop all that happening when we kid ourselves we like smoking, but nevertheless smokers do just that, then they relegate that work to the unconscious mind in the form of a learned concept. Just another book in the mental library, [another program in the bio-computer] to help us perceive that we like smoking.

Then we kid ourselves that to have a cigarette in our mouths makes us look older and more mature, or even 'macho'. Or we kid ourselves that cigarette smoking helps us to relax and be less tense, or soothe our nerves.. It is a well accepted fact that cigarette smoke is a chronic irritant and doesn't soothe nerves, but irritates to such an extent that the lungs will produce cancer, or bronchitis, or emphysema in an attempt to relieve that irritation. Additionally we may absorb toxins into our blood stream from the smoke that will increase our chances of heart, and blood vessel, disease. Our mouth, or throat, or stomach may respond to that smoky irritant and as a result, produce cancer of any of those areas.

Some years ago I remember an advert on the television which showed a person smoking a brand of cigarettes called 'Strand' The advert said 'You are never alone with a Strand.' Another showed a person who was smoking, get the best looking girl. The one smoking was made to look much more attractive to the other sex. The people making the advert knew just how to make you want to smoke. Their psychology was excellent.

I once was helping a friend to stop smoking and he got down to only one cigar a day. He said when he got out of bed he fancied a smoke, and sometimes he would be able to have his breakfast first. Sometimes he would even be able to get to work before he had to smoke, but before he did any work he had to have a cigar. The problem with smoking is that it is 'an all or nothing' thing. If you try just to cut down, you will end up smoking as many, or even more than you did before. So my friend and I both felt we should try to find out why he had to have his first and only cigar each day. In a state of hypnosis I asked his mind if it would help us to know why he had to have his first cigar? and to respond with an ideo-motor finger response. His finger rose, indicating its willingness to help us with our request. I asked if we could know when he first learned the behaviour which made him have to smoke that cigar and on a backward count from his present age we got to 0 before his finger rose. He became very excited and offered the information that when he was born he was very ill and was placed in an incubator, and drip fed. When he had recovered, his mother's milk had dried up and he had to be bottled fed. His mother had often told him this in his later life. *[Probably to relieve some guilt feelings she had about not breast feeding him.]* He continued by saying 'I never had her breast, so could that be the reason why I have to have a cigar when I wake up. I explained that waking up is like being born, so we asked his unconscious mind if it would raise his ideo-motor finger, if that was the dynamic factor in his having to have a cigarette in the morning before he could start work. His finger rose up quite quickly. After thanking his mind for trying to help him to cope with the repressed pain of not getting his mother's breast, by making him want to smoke on waking, I explained that this behaviour was just symbolic and not helpful, and anyhow he has a beautiful wife who loves him. So I asked his mind if it would now help him in another way without making him want to smoke and it indicated its willingness by raising his finger. He stopped smoking, and his wife was also quite pleased. I am not claiming this as proof of a dynamic factor in smoking but my friend succeeded in doing what he wanted. He now has more options about smoking in the morning.

We sometimes kid ourselves that we can think, or concentrate better with a cigarette, so when that difficult phone call comes through, or we have to do something that we need to concentrate about we light up a cigarette. Just another confidence trick, we do this because we have learned to reduce our anxiety by smoking, which is part of the oral gratification we learned very shortly after birth. If we think about it, we need oxygen in our brain to think clearly. If we smoke we are burning the oxygen out of the air we breathe so we have less. If we were to sit working in a room with a gas fire burning up the oxygen from the room, and if the room were sealed so that no more air could get in, fairly soon we would get a headache due to the lack of oxygen, and find it difficult to concentrate. We have to work hard at telling ourselves smoking helps us to concentrate, because it doesn't do that at all. Again, we can soon relegate that behaviour to our unconscious, just another book in the library of our mind, [another program in our bio-computer] to con ourselves we like smoking, and it helps us to concentrate.

Yet another con is to kid ourselves we belong with our friends by engaging in like behaviour and smoking with them. Do we really think our friends won't like us, or be our friends if we don't smoke? I have never smoked and I have never found any difficulty in making friends, even with those people who smoke. I have sometimes found it difficult to want to be friends with people who smoke constantly, because I find their smoking irritates my lungs and makes my eyes smart. Smoking is anti-social and often offends people who don't smoke, so if you don't smoke you are being far more considerate towards your friends and can 'belong' even more.

Some people even kid themselves they like the smell of cigarette smoke. Have you ever gone into a room that hasn't been aired, where someone has been smoking the night before. If you are a smoker do this before you light your first cigarette of the day. The whole room stinks, but quite quickly if you are a smoker you don't notice the smell. Once again in the beginning you have to work hard at not noticing the smell, but, again, fairly soon you can relegate that behaviour to your unconscious and go on offending your friends who don't smoke without even being aware that you are doing so. The smell doesn't go away, you just stop noticing it. My wife who doesn't smoke either, always tells me my clothes smell when I have been for a drink in a smoky pub. So not only does smoking not make it any easier to make friends, but it is also quite offensive to those friends who don't smoke.

To smoke you have to work very hard, at first, to kid yourselves you like smoking but when you have relegated that behaviour to your unconscious mind you still go on with the con without even noticing it. The con exists for a lot of unconscious reasons, but mainly because of doubts about yourself. There are much better ways, and much less harmful ways, of dealing with those doubts without having to resort to smoking. Don't ever kid yourself it's just a habit. It would be much easier to give it up if it was. So how do we go about helping someone to stop smoking?

TREATMENT IN CASES OF SMOKING.

First of all you can't stop someone from smoking who doesn't want to stop. It's no good trying to help someone because their doctor says they must give it up, or because their wife, or husband, or parent, says they should. If the person doesn't really want to give up smoking you have no chance. So first of all you must make quite sure who it is that wants to stop smoking. If the patient wants to stop, then I try to shift the responsibility from me, to them, by asking them if they can, from right now, consider themselves a non-smoker. I tell them if they will do this I will help them be just that. It is very difficult to stop someone doing something they want to do, it is much easier to help someone to be something they want. So if they want to be a non-smoker it is much easier to do that, than stopping them from smoking. If they really want to be a non-smoker, every cigarette they smoke, from now is giving up what they want to be. All this may seem to be hair splitting but it is extremely important to have as many concepts working for you, especially in your unconscious mind, when there are probably quite a few concepts working against you. By first explaining the above principles to the patient you are beginning to put some books about being a non-smoker into their unconscious mind. They already have too many about smoking to make it easy.

For instance there may be a book saying it is mature, grown up, adult, or even 'macho' to smoke. Another may say it relaxes you, makes you less tense, or even soothes your nerves to smoke. Another tells you that you like the taste of smoking, it helps you to think, or concentrate, or even gives you confidence because you are more grown-up smoking. Even another may be telling you that you 'belong' more when you smoke. All these books were written when you first started smoking and you had to work very hard to make them work. Once you did, however, you then relegated them to your unconscious mind, and they still go on working for you as dynamic processes without you even being aware of them. So if you are trying to stop smoking, all the books mentioned in this paragraph are working against your efforts and will cause conflicts which may defeat you.

To 'try' suggests it may be difficult, and you may fail. To have to 'give something up' suggests you want to do that which you are trying to give up. Both 'try' and 'give up' are negative thoughts, as is 'will power'. Many people ask you to give them more 'will power' to give up. That really means I want you to make me give up something I really want to do, and no way can you do that. If, on the other hand, your patient wants to be a non-smoker, to help him achieve what he wants is increasing his want power and that is positive. The point of all therapy is to become more positive and do what you want, not to give up what you want.

If patients are not too sure about being able to consider themselves non-smokers from right now, then I ask them if there is a time in the future when they might be able to do that. If there is such a time in the future, then I make an appointment at that time in the future. In the meantime while they are waiting for that time to come, I ask them not to ever smoke the same brand of cigarettes so that they have to smoke different brands. I do this because they all have their favourite brand, and if they have to smoke other brands which they don't like, they are beginning not to like smoking so much and will be more ready to become a non-smoker when the appointed time arrives.

During the awaited period they could also have a non-smoking time. For instance they could refrain from smoking for the first two hours after they get up in the morning, and then every few days extend the time by one hour more in which they didn't smoke. This is helping them to see it can be easier to become a non—smoker when the time comes. Or they could develop a non-smoking place, for instance they could not smoke in their home, or at work, or both these places, which again would show them that if they could not need to smoke in either of those two places it would be easy to not smoke anywhere, and be a non-smoker.

It is also useful to ask the smoker when they had their first cigarette, and what were the circumstances? Why did they smoke that first cigarette? The answer to these questions may give a clue to the unconscious dynamic factors in their uncontrollable habit. After all if they have to come to a hypnotist to help them, something must be making them have to smoke, otherwise they would just stop. It is also useful to ask them if there are any times in the present when they feel a stronger urge to smoke? The answers to this question will give you a clue to any 'anchor situations' that they are likely to encounter. [Anchor situations are times and places where they have been accustomed to smoking, like smoking when they have a pint, or after an enjoyable meal, or just before they make a difficult telephone call etc.] If we look at smoking adverts on television they are nearly all connected with some 'anchor situation' because the adver- tisers know how important these situations really are. [A castella and a pint] They also often link them with some macho situation as once again they know how we kid ourselves. (They show some man getting a beautiful girl as a result of smoking.] Yet it is surprising how many uncon-

scious minds will pick up that clue without the conscious
ever even noticing.

So now let us assume we have a person who is ready to
consider themselves a non-smoker, and let us look at a series
of exercises to assist them in achieving that goal.

EXERCISE 18.
Using ideo-motor finger questioning as described on page 21,
ask the unconscious mind if it feels more mature or adult or
even 'macho' smoking cigarettes? If yes, reframe that by
showing the unconscious mind that it is much more mature,
adult and even more macho to rely on oneself instead of a
stick of dried up leaves which one sets alight to 'KID' oneself.
Tell yourself it is not mature or 'macho' to con yourself.

EXERCISE 19.
If the ideo-motor finger rises to the question,' does cigarette
smoking make you more relaxed, less tense, or soothe your
nerves', then you must reframe that book in the library of the
unconscious by explaining that smoking is irritating to the
extent of causing serious health risks and there are much
better ways of feeling relaxed than conning oneself. Tell
yourself smoking is irritating not relaxing.

EXERCISE 20.
If smoking helps you to concentrate you must reframe that by
telling yourself that smoking burns the oxygen out of the air
that you breathe so that your brain is starved of oxygen and is
less efficient, so smoking makes concentration worse, not
better.

EXERCISE 21.
If smoking helps you to belong, reframe that by telling
yourself that there are more people now who don't smoke,
so smoking is anti-social and smelly and irritating to
non-smokers and as you are now a non-smoker you are
letting yourself down and giving up what you want to be by
smoking, so you don't want to smoke.

EXERCISE 22.

[SPIEGEL'S BODY IMAGE.] Tell yourself when you are in a state of hypnosis that your body is your most valuable and precious possession. Cigarette smoke is poison to your body. You are going to give your body the consideration and concern it deserves. Your body is much more valuable to you than your home or car. If you were going to manure your roses you wouldn't put the manure on your best carpet or on the back seat of your car, yet your body is much more valuable to you than your carpet or back seat of your car. Cigarette smoke is more damaging to your body than manure is to your home, so you will give as much if not more respect to your body as you can't change your body, you can change your car, or carpet.

EXERCISE 23.

[SPIEGEL'S SPLIT SCREEN] While you are in a relaxed state of hypnosis and you feel your mind floating, create an image of a screen on the other side of the room divided down the middle. On one side of the screen have an image of yourself smoking and doing all sorts of damage to your body by so doing. On the other side of the screen have an image of yourself being a non-smoker, giving your body the con- sideration and concern it deserves, and choose and tell your mind which 'You' you want to be. Bring back from the screen the 'You' you want to be, leaving the 'You' you don't want on the other side of the room. Integrate the 'You' you want by feeling how it would be to be a non-smoker. Then just open your eyes and be a non-smoker.

EXERCISE 24.

For patients who have young children who don't like you smoking. Place a picture of your children into the packet of cigarettes that you are currently carrying where it will be seen as soon as you open the packet. When you see the picture of your children [child] ask yourself if you want to set your children an example they might not be able to resist, and result in you being responsible for them getting cancer. Do you need a cigarette more than the example you could set your children? Ask the patient if they find themselves getting in some ways more like their parents in spite of themselves. Nearly everyone does find in some way they get more like their parents even in those ways they don't admire in their parents.

I was asked to help a man who had a young daughter who hated his smoking. His wife had died of lung cancer due to smoking, so naturally his fifteen-year-old daughter didn't want to lose him too. He had tried to give up unsuccessfully so I asked him to put a photograph of his daughter in his packet of cigarettes and he never smoked another cigarette.

Do at least one of the above exercises every two to three hours of your waking day, spending no more than two minutes on the exercise until you have no desire to con yourself any more about smoking, and you are happy to be a non-smoker. If someone should offer you a cigarette say 'no thank you I don't smoke'. Don't say 'I have given it up'. If you say 'I have given it up', you may well cause some guilt feelings in the person offering you the cigarette as they most probably have at some time thought they should give it up, and been unsuccessful. They may well try to relieve their own guilt by trying to persuade you to smoke. It is hard enough, without smoking to relieve someone elses guilt. If you say 'I don't smoke', most people will accept that without feeling guilty.

Don't be tempted to substitute smoking with another form of oral gratification. Over-eating is the most common way people try to overcome smoking and then they have to start to smoke to lose weight. This substitute is just another way we have for cheating on ourselves. I once read in a hypnotic journal a case history where the hypnotist was recommending to the patient that they should reward themselves for not smoking by having a box of chocolates. I wondered if they returned for treatment for smoking and over-weight? It is always better to suggest at sometime in the hypnotic treatment that the patient will not be tempted to over eat as a substitute.

Remember it is almost impossible to cut down on smoking, it is an 'all-or-nothing' thing. Don't be tempted in an 'anchor situation' to just have one cigarette, it won't end there. Every time you resist an 'anchor situation' without smoking, the anchor will get weaker. It may be necessary to help someone to cope with 'anchor situations' by taking them through the situation in hypnotic dream or enactment and seeing themselves still being a non—smoker. If all or any of the above exercises don't work, then it will probably be necessary to find out exactly why the patient needs to smoke. If one thing doesn't work in hypnosis then do something else, don't just keep on doing the same old thing hoping that eventually it may work.

I once was asked to help a man to be a non-smoker who managed to override all attempts to help him. In the end he admitted he didn't really want to stop smoking he really wanted to see if he could trust me to help him with another much more personal and private problem. I did help him with that problem and he is much happier but still smokes. You have no right to tell people what they should do unless they ask for help. This presents the main difficulty in treating children smokers, most of them don't want to stop. They refuse to admit they are addicted and until they do there is very little anyone can do. Most of them even refuse to talk about smoking, and if you try to get them to talk, they become very defensive, which only goes to show how much their unconscious mind really needs the dynamic processes discussed in this chapter connected with the habit of smoking. Most parents also seem to refuse to take any responsibility for their childrens' behaviour and pass the buck onto the schools. [See next chapter on alcohol and drug taking.]

CHAPTER 3

Alcoholism. Can we stop drinking to excess?

Alcoholism, like any drug addiction, is very difficult to treat. Most alcoholics, like all addicts, require expert help. One of the main problems is the addict's utter dependency, whether it be on alcohol or any other drug. This makes it very difficult to get the patient's total co-operation, both in wanting to give it up and in the treatment necessary to assist them to kick the habit. This dependency is both physical and psychological, although I believe a lot of the physical symptoms are the mind's way of persuading the person they need their drug and don't really want to give it up. I also feel with the right help the physical symptoms of withdrawal can be greatly reduced.

Many addictions start while the patient is still a child at school. Again the main difficulty in treating this ever growing problem is the refusal of the patient to see the problem in the first place, and their refusal to admit they are addicted, indicated by their saying 'I could stop now if I wanted to', which, by the way, is also a way of saying 'I don't want to stop now'. Their refusal to accept the damage that their particular addiction will have on their health, even when everyone else can see a gross deterioration in their physical well-being, only goes to show how hard they have had to work at liking their habit; and how they have now relegated that work to their unconscious mind so that they can go on with the habit to get the so called benefits they have conned themselves into believing they get, **and unconsciously need**, from continuing with the addiction. *[Some very strong books have to be created in their conceptual* *library, [strong programs in their bio-computer] to do this, which they defend at all costs, even sometimes to the death.]*

Again, like the smoking habit, parents seem to be getting into a distinct panic about the apparent failure of schools to deal with the alarming growth in the addiction problem. I say it is not the schools' responsibility, it is the parents' denial of their responsibility long ago, that has created the need for the child to resort to drugs in the first place. By the time a child resorts to drugs to boost its ego, the parent has long since lost the ability to be a parent to that child, and in the first instance they deny their child is taking drugs or alcohol to relieve their own guilt as a parent in letting their child down. Secondly, the parent can't understand why the child doesn't listen to their warnings about alcohol or other drugs, when long ago that parent lost the ability to communicate with its children. It is marvellous how parents push their children's needs aside to concentrate on their own material needs and comfort, and then can't understand when their child takes no notice of them when they later find it necessary to give them advice. In their exasperation at being unable to get across to their children at times of need, they then transfer their own responsibility totally to the schools to relieve their own guilt. *[To get some ideas of what your child needs, see my first book on* **'How to be the Parent You Never Had'**]

I also believe that the great increase in violence, vandalism, robbery and petty crime among teenagers is directly contributed to, by the break up of family life, and of an extension of family life in the community. There is now a large number of families where both parents have to go out to work, and a general debasing of the importance of the job of being a housewife, so that housewives feel second class citizens. Because of this, I feel sure that the basic needs of the children are being increasingly neglected. This is resulting in the alarming increase in the number of children turning to smoking, alcoholism, drug taking, and crime and a general lack of consideration for other people's property and possessions, and even a lack of concern in their own health, as a defence against their own needs being neglected.

Vandalism and hooliganism are not, as has often been

suggested, a **result** of an increase in alcohol consumption, or drug taking, they are all **symptoms** of the same thing and a result of the break down of the family unit. The long-term cure is somehow to restore family life, and the respectability and importance of being good parents in bringing up children; to avoid losing contact in communication with ones' children and to both teach by example and give love to each other. How to do that is a 'billion dollar question'.

Unemployment may have something to do with the break up of family life, but it is only secondary to that break up, which is primarily the cause of the teenage problem today.

How do we go about treating alcoholism when we have a patient who both wants treatment and admits they are addicted, which is partly the same thing. To admit one is addicted is admitting one needs help and treatment. Not to admit addiction is really saying 'I could give it up but I don't want to yet'. Remember it is very nearly impossible to make someone give up something they don't want to.

Treatment of Alcoholism.

My first question to any addict, regardless of age, is 'can you cuddle both of your parents affectionately?' [See my first book **'How to become the Parent you never Had'**] I have yet to meet an addict who can do that simple task, showing a breakdown somewhere in communication between one, or both parents, and the addict. If they can't cuddle either, or both parents ask them 'why not?' The answer to that question should give you a clue to some of the hurt that may be partly responsible for the addiction. Then ask them 'are there any other problems in your life right now that you have difficulty in handling?' If there are, then the answers may give you some more clues as to the hurt that the alcohol helps to deaden. Next ask them 'why do you think you have to drink?' The most common answer is 'it helps me to relax, or cope'. This means I can't relax, or cope, without alcohol. Really it means 'I have chosen alcohol to relax me, or to help me to cope with my life'. There are always alternative ways of relaxing, or coping with life, the alcoholic just hasn't seen any. The therapists job is to convince his patient, first of all that there are options, and of the advantages of the alternatives. The patient must also be taught how to become the parent they never had. [**See my earlier book.**]

The next question is 'what sort of person do you think you are?' Most alcoholics have a very poor opinion of themselves. Their answers to the above question will give you more clues as to the hurts that alcohol helps them cope with. It also gives a clue as to the value the alcoholic puts on their life. Again most alcoholics don't put much value on their life, and often death is a considered option to not drinking, or drinking themselves to death is the easiest way out. The therapist must be aware of the value the alcoholic puts on his life and the dangers and difficulties that a low esteem will produce. It is very necessary in the treatment of addictions to build the esteem of the patient by the therapist showing concern and respect for the patient. If, as a therapist, you can't do that, then you shouldn't be treating patients at all, never mind alcoholics.

Another important question is 'can you show, and express your feelings easily without alcohol?' Most alcoholics can't, so they take alcohol to be nearer to their feelings without having to feel them, because the alcohol stops them from having to feel their hurt. They can 'feel' their feelings under the 'anaesthetic' that alcohol provides. The trouble often is that their feelings have nothing to do with what is going on at this moment, but has to do with some past hurt, so that their behaviour is relevant to that past hurt, and not to the present. This often results in quite unreasonable behaviour like violence, abusive behaviour or behaviour which will result in the person being even further removed from their 'real needs' of now. It also leads to the person having an even lower opinion of themselves so they have to drink more not to feel guilty. If alcoholic's can't show and express their feelings without alcohol they have to be taught to 'feel their real feelings of now' without resorting to alcohol. Once again they have options but the alcoholic hasn't seen any. They must be taught that past hurts are over, and there are better ways of coping with the present than being anaesthetized. [See my case history of 'Bill' in my first book **'How to Become** the Parent You Never Had', chapter three page 29-30]

Amanda was referred to me by her doctor for alcoholism. She was thirty-five years old and was drinking very heavily and was unable to stop. I asked her to write her history from as early as she could remember to the present day, with any reasons she could give for her drinking. Her account follows in full with my own comments in italics.

'I was born the youngest of seven children and I can remember many happy things in my childhood, in fact in many ways I think I was overindulged but I can never remember a time when there was not an 'atmosphere' in our home. *[You have to believe it's happy even if it isn't, how can it be happy with a bad atmosphere always present?]* The only way I can explain 'atmosphere' is that there always seemed to be a cover-up of true feelings. We were not a demonstrative family as far as affection was concerned but I certainly don't think that affection did not exist between us, it was just sort of covered up. *[love has to be felt by physical contact, by emotional contact and by intellectual contact if it is to be any good. She could not cuddle either of her parents showing the absence of real love]* For instance, my mother had such lovely soft skin on her face, sometimes I used to touch it but I always longed to kiss it, as I had seen some of my friends do to their mothers but that just wasn't done in our family. *[What a pity. It would have been so much better if it had]*

The house in which I was born was very small—far too small to accommodate nine people but my maiden aunt lived across the street from us and the three older children slept there. My other aunt on my mother's side lived more comfortably round the corner with her husband and three children. My aunts thought my mother had married below her station and as a result treated her as a third-class citizen, which my mother accepted until towards the end of her life. She was always having to run after them and she cooked for my maiden aunt as she went out to work. The fact that my aunts disliked my father didn't make life easy for any of us.

I am told as a small child I was very fond of my father. *[If you have to be told to know, it didn't exist, or was destroyed long ago]* This confuses me as I can never remember having any affection for him. In fact my first memory of physical contact with him made me uneasy and even to this day I feel the same. *[No way can she cuddle him now]* Somehow I have deep down associated him with the 'atmosphere' in our home. Everyone who visited our house thought he was such a charming man which he really was to outsiders, and incidentally we were always encouraged to bring our friends home. *[Many people wear a mask to outsiders and don't show their true self]* However only the family saw the other side of him—bad tempered, self centred and a terrible bully when he could get away with it. *[Probably due to his own childhood. The sins of the fathers visit the children]* When I was about five years old we moved into a larger house but two of my brothers were in a sanatorium with T.B. My other brother had also quit college and things weren't too happy at home. This brother was going to marry a non-Catholic, and as we were all Catholics you can imagine the atmosphere this created. He eventually left home and married but there was no reconciliation and his three children were never accepted. My mother never showed any feelings over this either, but I'm sure she was heart-broken. *[It just goes to show how extremes of anything (in this case religion) spoil love and screw people up]* Meantime both my two other brothers were discharged from hospital, and it is roughly about this time that my first real memories of unhappiness and tension surfaced. *[She could not deny it any longer.)* I think these can be directed in three ways.

1. My aunt and mother spoiled me a lot and, like most mothers with their youngest child, tended to keep me a baby as long as possible. The result was that the two children nearest to me in age wouldn't let me be close to them. They were obviously jealous of me and thought I was mother's 'pet' and a 'cry baby'. I don't remember being a particularly tearful child but their mocking did reduce me to tears. However I became determined not to cry in the hope that they would accept me. I did learn not to cry almost permanently but it didn't achieve my aim to any great extent. *[No, it only taught you not to feel and you are still doing that with*

alcohol.]

2. When my brother came home from hospital I soon became very afraid of him. He always seemed so harsh with me and try as I would I never seemed to be able to gain his approval. The gap between us was so wide and my confidence so diminished that I was incapable of bridging it. *[If you don't feel loved by your parents you have to get love from someone else, and if you fail there, then you are really in trouble because you don't like yourself and blame yourself for being unlovable.]* If only I had been able to, I think he would have been a great help to me. *[There you go, blaming yourself]* His own education was terminated through his ill health and he was determined that we would make the most of ours, so he made himself responsible for supervising our homework and scrutinising our school reports, and of course even when I was top of the class there were no pats on the back. *[It is equally important if you wish to help someone that you give praise as well as criticism, otherwise the person never learns to believe in themselves no matter what they do. They have to stop feeling, to cope, and Amanda is doing that now with alcohol]*

3. I think the third and worst part of my young life was caused by constant weekly quarrels between my mother and father over his Saturday night drinking. Every Saturday night followed the same pattern, and being the youngest I was always the only one left in with my mother. I remember I always sat with my tummy in knots and my hands hot and sticky watching the clock tick round to quarter to ten. Funnily enough, my father never got really drunk but alcohol always loosened his tongue and when he came in he never stopped talking. There was, of course, an ensuing row but never any violence until that one time when I was fourteen. Despite the fact that I preferred my mother to my father, I always prayed that she wouldn't start when he came in, but rather humour him, but after all these years she had very little humour for him. In her younger days he used to go out every night and now she felt that he might at least take her out now and again but he was too selfish for that. In fact only once he took my mother and my sister and I to a film and he left us in the

cinema so that he could catch the pub before closing time, so it wasn't really a very happy outing.

My sister was five years older than me and I adored her. In fact everyone thought a lot of her. She had turned into a very beautiful young girl but she also developed a very cold nature. She really only loved one person and that was herself. *[Amanda's sister has also stopped feeling, which is hardly surprising but she defends by only believing in herself.]* When my sister was about fourteen she began to worry my mother. She would not come in at a reasonable time so my mother had to put sanctions on her which she usually ignored. This was usually on a Friday night and so I found myself sitting tense and miserable on both Friday and Saturday nights. *[She is learning to be tense even without doing anything herself, just another book in her mental library.]*.

The result of my sister's behaviour caused a lack of trust between my mother and her and thus my mother placed a lot more responsibility on me, making me have to grow up very quickly. As I pointed out before she had previously kept me a child for so long. I found the only way I could accept these things with any confidence was to pretend, but underneath I was really frightened. I had to keep up the pretence in the years to come until it became too much for me and I found my escape in alcohol.'

In Amanda's treatment we had to work through the hate she felt for her father and try to show her that he was probably the way he was because of his own childhood. This meant it was not her fault her father couldn't show her he loved her. We also had to work through the disappointment she felt in her mother not being able to show her feelings towards her. This again was probably due to her mother's childhood and not because Amanda was unlovable.

Obviously her brothers and sisters had the same treatment as Amanda so they had also stopped feeling, and couldn't show her any love, so try as she may, she was doomed to failure in any attempts she might make in that direction. Once again, not because she was unlovable but because they couldn't show any feelings. In her attempts to get their love she had become a 'dogsbody' to their every wish. She would go and sleep with her sister whenever her sister's husband was away from home, because her sister was afraid to be on her own. She was just as afraid but had to pretend she wasn't. Still her sister couldn't show her any love.

We had to work through the resentment she felt at her brother always criticising her every behaviour, and show her that that was the only way he knew of showing his concern for her. It was his way of showing he loved her, and the only way he knew how. It was sad that he knew no better way of showing her that he cared but what was, was, and he couldn't help it.

We then had to show her there was no love to be found in alcohol, nor would it make her feel any more secure, nor would it fill any emptiness at not being loved. We had to work through the anger she felt for her family in always involving her in their troubles, and once again show her that that was the only way they could show her that they loved her. We had to show her that they were just as afraid of love as she was, and they all had found their own way of coping with that.

We had to teach her that she would have to learn to give herself the love her parents had been unable to give her. [**To become the parent she never had. See my first book**] Alcohol would never be able to do that and she would learn to feel real feelings again. All this gave her new options. It took some thirty-five visits over two years. You will note that I use the term we in therapy, meaning the patient and I, as all treatment is a joint commitment between therapist and patient.

The way in which addictions reduce one's options in life must be fully explained to the patient and how, with reduced options, happiness will evade them. The journey of life becomes frustrated and through alcohol or drugs, they will never reach that higher plane in life that is the very purpose of life itself. [**See my first book.**]

Each addict must be treated individually according to their needs, and the following exercises are not intended to replace individual treatment, but to augment that treatment by giving the patient something to do for themselves between treatment sessions.

EXERCISE 25.
Treatment of Alcoholism by N.L.P. Reframing.

Find out which situations make you drink. *[What are the 'Anchor' situations which make you want to drink?]* When you know all the situations in which you would normally want to drink then enter the hypnotic state as in Exercise 1. Start with the first situation and create an image of yourself in that situation and be very positive in your mind that drinking will not help, but only make it worse and compound your difficulties. Ask your mind to find another way of helping you to cope with that situation without making you want to drink. Repeat this exercise with all the situations in which you normally would resort to drink and ask your mind to find other ways of helping you.

Having done this, set up an ideo-motor finger response as in Exercise 2. and ask the part of your mind that makes you drink, when it is listening, paying attention, wanting to help you and is willing to negotiate, to lift your 'Yes' finger high in the air. When your finger lifts, ask it if it willing to let you know what secondary gain is achieved by drinking. [i.e. confidence, relaxation, relief of any form of pain,(physical or psychological), camaraderie, relief from guilt, etc.] If it is willing, let it lift your 'Yes' finger. If it is not willing to let you know what the secondary gain is, let it lift your 'No' finger.

If your 'Yes' finger lifts ask it to let your mind know now what the secondary gain is. If your 'No' finger lifts then just go on to the next part without knowing. It is more helpful if you know what the gain is consciously, but if your mind is unwilling to let you know now it is generally due to a poor ego image *[a low opinion of your self that may be made even worse if you have to know consciously what the secondary gain is, you receive from drinking.]* Your unconscious mind knows what the gain is otherwise it couldn't produce that gain unconsciously for you. You should on no account try to force your mind to reveal anything it feels uncomfortable about. You may find as you get stronger your mind will willingly disclose the gain at a later time. In either case go on to the next part of this exercise described below.

Now find another part of your mind that can help you achieve the same secondary gain, without having to resort to drink. When you have found another part that will help you achieve the same gain without producing the damage that alcohol does, ask it to get together with the part that makes you drink, and persuade the part that makes you drink to help you in this new and better way. Ask both parts if they will produce the secondary gain in this new and better way in all the situations that in the past would have made you resort to drink. When they feel confident that they will now help you in this better way let them both lift your 'Yes' finger. You don't have to know consciously what this better way is for it to work.

A person will always make the best choice available to him or her in any situation. Before this reframing your mind didn't realise it had a choice. You have just shown it there are better ways of coping. If you offer your mind better choices than drinking to get all the positive secondary gains of alcohol, your mind will make the better selections, and you can stop having to drink.

It is very possible that the above exercise will have to be done with a therapist for the first few times as it may be difficult to remember all of the exercise on your own, especially when your eyes are shut, and a therapist can suit the treatment to your individual needs and 'Anchor' situations. Remember every time you resist an 'Anchor' situation the 'Anchor' becomes weaker.

This exercise, and the following ones can all be used for any addiction. Just substitute, for alcohol, which ever drug you are addicted to, in any of these exercises.

EXERCISE 26.
[SPIEGEL'S SPLIT SCREEN.] While you are in a relaxed state of hypnosis and feel your mind floating, create an image of a screen on the other side of the room, divided down the middle. On one side of the screen have an image of yourself drinking and doing all sorts of damage to your body and mind by being drunk, and being obnoxious as a result of

being intoxicated. On the other side of the screen have an image of yourself not drinking at all, giving your body and mind and friends the consideration and concern they deserve. See how much clearer you can think and behave, and how much you prefer this you. Tell your mind which 'You' you want to be, and bring back from the screen the 'You' you want to be, leaving the 'You' you don't want on the other side of the room. Integrate the 'You' you want by feeling how it is, to not drink, then open your eyes and don't drink.

For treatment of other drug addictions, substitute the other drug for alcohol

EXERCISE 27.

[SPIEGEL'S BODY IMAGE.] Tell yourself when you are in a state of hypnosis that your body and mind are your most valuable and precious possessions. Alcohol [or other drug] is poison to your body and mind. You are going to give your body and mind the consideration and concern it deserves. Open your eyes and give your body and mind that consideration.

Do these last two exercises every two to three hours for two minutes at a time during your waking hours, until you no longer want to drink alcohol, [or take the drug], and repeat if ever your desire to drink, [or take the drug] returns.

CHAPTER 4.

Oral sex. Does it do any harm?

There are two distinct and very different forms of sexual behaviour. For the sake of description in this chapter let us call the first one 'making love'. When two people are making love each one is doing something to please the other simultaneously. Each one is surrendering self to please the other, in an attempt to become as one. It is like the cosmic consciousness we experience in the womb. [**See my first book.**] It is almost like a womb return. It is not two people doing separate things to each other, but two people becoming one with each other. Two people becoming one with the room they are in, becoming one with the house the room is in, becoming one with the country the house is in, becoming one with the world the country is in. It is a surrender of self and ego to feeling. At the point of orgasm there is a total release of tension to feeling, and being at one with the world and every thing in it.

Provided both persons involved are old enough to know what they are doing, and are willing participants in everything that they are doing with each other, then there should be nothing that is taboo, no part of their bodies 'dirty'. Everything is, and should be, permissible, without guilt, bad feeling or disgrace. There is, and should be, nothing more beautiful, than two people telling, and showing, the other that they love each other with their bodies in a surrender of one to the other. Even in the marriage ceremony there is the oath which is said to each other, before God, and the congregation 'With my body I thee honour'. That should mean exactly what I have written above. Oral sex in the above context is not dirty, disgraceful, taboo or harmful.

49

In the act of making love it is most likely that both people involved will find that their bodies and organs work without failure, as neither is trying to prove anything, but each is just giving the other pleasure. There are many people who would find it too dangerous to make love and desperately need to hang on to self, for fear of losing self. These people indulge in the second form of sexual behaviour.

Let us call the second form of sexual behaviour 'fucking'. When two people fuck each other, two people are doing separate things to each other, each for personal reasons, and neither losing themselves in the other. Generally, each is desperately hanging on to self, often trying to prove something. It is common for either, or both, to ask the other when they have finished 'Was I good?' or 'Was it good?' Sometimes they even award points out of ten for performance. It is common in this form of sexual behaviour for one, or both partners, to experience some difficulties at some time in their life, due to the over importance they put on the act. Many people can only behave in this manner, as to 'make love', as described above, would present too much danger. These are the people who have been hurt at one time, generally by their parents, by wanting love and not getting it.

Some people indulge in both forms of sexual behaviour at different times. I am sure many of you reading this chapter will recognize both forms, in your own behaviour. Once again, provided that both partners are old enough to know what they are doing, and both are willing participants in everything that they are doing to the other, then everything is, and should be, acceptable. Nothing is dirty, disgraceful or disgusting. There is no harm in oral sex provided both partners are totally willing.

If, on the other hand, one partner is not willing, as in rape, then this form of sexual behaviour can, and does, have a very bad effect on the unwilling party.

When a child is persuaded by a relative or 'called relative' to have sexual behaviour, or is assaulted by an adult, the effect can be, and often is, disastrous on the child, and subsequent adult. One of the problems in this form of sexual behaviour is that the child often trusts the parent or relative or called 'uncle' and innocently participates without realizing what is happening until it is too late. In this case, when it subsequently realizes what it has done, it is devastated by guilt, even though at the time it was guiltless.

When a child indulges in oral sex, before it is old enough to know what it is doing, or even when an adult is forced to have oral sex against their wishes, the effect is often very harmful.

On the 10th. of August 1980 Dorothy Bestford was referred to me, suffering from a long standing Anxiety Depression. She had first been diagnosed as depressive shortly after the birth of her son who was now sixteen years old, but she had had bouts of feeling 'bad' [as she put it] for as long as she could remember. Her account of her life is shown in full below.

'I was born in 1940 and until 1949 I thought I was the eldest of three children. I don't remember much of my early childhood, but I think I was very unhappy but don't know why. I think my two younger brothers were cruel to me but again I can't remember how. I think my father was also cruel to me and I am still afraid of him now, but I don't know why. I don't ever remember my mother being loving towards me. *[If your childhood is painful or unhappy the tendency is to forget it if you can. If you can't remember your mother being loving towards you she most probably wasn't loving.]* When I was nine years old my aunt took me away from my parents but I didn't know why at the time. Nobody seemed to want to tell me anything, except I got the impression that I had done something very wrong that no one ever talked about. I felt very guilty at the time, but I don't know why.

My aunt told me just before she died, when I was fourteen, that she was actually my real mother, and not my aunt, and the lady I thought was my mother was really my aunt. My real parents were very poor and had three children before me and at that time my real aunt had not been able to have any children. My real mother gave me to my aunt immediately after my birth so that is why I thought my aunt was my mother. My real aunt subsequently had two children of her own, which is often the case after adoption. My real mother never told my why she took me back when I was nine.

When I was given all this information I was very confused at the time, and even today I don't really know who I am. At least I do now know who I am, but I still feel very confused. My real mother said they could not keep me at birth because their house was full up, and they couldn't really afford another child. I don't understand how they could have given me away. I was very shocked when she told me, but she was very ill, and shortly afterwards she died. My real father was very unhappy and upset at her death and he couldn't talk to me. My real elder brother [the one born immediately before me] was close to me and he did talk to me but not about my childhood. I didn't feel a lot about my real mother's death because I had never got to know her properly.

I didn't get on with my other real brother and sister and I still don't like them, so I don't feel I belong anywhere. [They probably felt put out and resented you when your parents brought you back home. They probably felt you didn't belong there either.] When I was eighteen my real brother, who I liked and got on with, was very depressed. One weekend I was out with my boyfriend and when I returned home I found my brother had killed himself by taking an overdose of tablets which, unknown to me, he had been saving up. My other brother and sister blamed me and I felt very guilty for a long time, I still do when I think about it. [Later, when we were in therapy, we discussed her brother and she burst into tears saying it was her fault.]

I felt really bad after my brother's death for a long time, and broke off my friendship with the boy I had been going out with at the time. [Proof of blaming herself]

When I was twenty-two my real father died, but I didn't feel as bad about that, because I had never got to know him either. I was going out with my present husband at the time and I married him shortly afterwards, I think to have somewhere to live. I don't really think that I loved him but I may have at the time. About a year and a half later my son was born, when I was twenty-four.

I was very depressed after a very difficult birth, and could not accept my son at the time, which was very upsetting. [A *woman giving birth often relives part of their own birth with their own birth feelings. Post natal depression is a feeling you felt at your own birth.* **See my first book.**] I felt very guilty about not being able to feel for my son. I also felt in some way I wanted to harm him. I have felt very frightened about this feeling and I still feel it sometimes even now. I have never done anything to harm him, but the feeling I might, is often with me, and makes me terrified and guilty. I was given anti-depressants by the psychiatrist but they just keep my feelings at bay. They never go right away. I felt bad, off and on from then on, and when my daughter was born eight years later I again was very depressed and even suicidal. Again I couldn't feel any love for my daughter and I also was terrified that I would in some way do her some harm. I never have harmed either of them who, incidentally, I love very much now.

I feel a very bad person and often wish I was dead. I feel nothing for my husband who is very understanding with me. I'm sure he loves me but he can't show his feelings either. He is a very considerate husband and a good provider and I'm sure I should love him but I feel nothing for him and feel guilty about that. I can't stand him to touch me so we don't ever sleep together. That's just dirty and I can't stand it. He seems to accept that so now he never tries anything, but sometimes he complains.

I am still taking pills from the psychiatrist and have tried a lot of different kinds, some of them improve my mood temporarily but none of them make me feel any better for very long. Most of the time I feel frightened about all sorts of things and of harming my children. All the time I feel bad and depressed. I feel I'm a very bad and wicked person and often wish I was dead. I have never done anything to harm myself, I'm too frightened to do that. I don't feel I belong anywhere and am very confused.

Please help me as I don't know how I am going to go on.' It took me quite a time to get all this information out of her.

You can imagine I felt a little apprehensive about taking on such a complicated case. Where do you begin with such a history? There seemed to be so many questions unanswered in her life. First of all what happened in her first nine years of her life that she had suppressed so much that she couldn't remember anything? How had her foster parents been cruel to her? Why did she still fear her father who really was her uncle? Why did her real mother take her back at nine years old? *[No wonder she was confused]* What happened that no one could talk about, and yet insinuate that somehow it was partly to do with Dorothy and she was in some way guilty? Why did her brother kill himself? and why did she feel guilty about that? Why did she want to harm her own children when she loved them? Why does she find sex dirty and disgusting? Why is she afraid of all sorts of things now? Why does she feel a bad person and guilty about everything? How do you make her feel she belongs to anything? and to what? What can be done about Dorothy not feeling that she loves her husband? At least if she loved him she could belong to him and her own children. Why did she get post natal depression after the birth of both her own children?

I think what made me decide to take her on as a patient was that beneath all this trouble there seemed a very nice person who desperately needed help to come out of her shell. I myself felt I could somehow respect her. It is essential that a therapist should feel that, otherwise how are they going to make the patient feel any self-respect? It is essential in the therapy that the patient gains self-respect, otherwise they will for ever have to depend on the therapist, and never really get better.

Dorothy was fortunately a high capacity hypnotic subject, which meant that at least we should be able to make some new concepts for her to perceive by. We should also be able to re-write some of her old concepts, and that way change her perception of herself to something more acceptable to herself. The first essential step was to try to establish some positive anchor feelings for Dorothy. I tried to do this by having her visualise the 'Marathon' she swam to be here. [**See my first book.**] I had her tell herself in an altered state of hypnosis that she asked to be here, that she had just as much right as anybody else to be here, that she could win and had already proved that by winning the marathon she had swam to be here. Then she was to tell herself that she will win in the journey of life so that she won't have to do it all over again. *(With her history of her early life this last exercise would be a big incentive for her to 'make it', as I felt sure she wouldn't like to go through all that again.]* Then she would begin to like herself for winning a marathon and eventually learn to love herself. **[See the exercises in my first book page 10 chapter one.]**

I then tried to get her to see that in spite of having feelings of wanting to hurt her children she never had hurt them and really was a very good mother and loved her children. No way could she have given her children away, as the fact that her mother had given her away seemed to hurt Dorothy a great deal. Using an ideo-motor finger signal we discovered that the feeling of wanting to hurt her children was a result of her children reminding Dorothy unconsciously of her own unhappy childhood. Unconsciously her children were making Dorothy feel the hurt of not having a mother who loved her enough to find a way of keeping her and making her feel loved. *[So what happened with her foster parents that they didn't make her feel loved? It is difficult to give someone else what you never had and always wanted for yourself, hence her feeling of resentment for her own children and her fear that she would harm them.]* We worked on her resentment, building a greater awareness of her feelings of love for her own two children. This seemed to help Dorothy have a better self image. I taught her to celebrate this better image by visualizing it often and feeling good about it.

She then said she felt so guilty about her brother's suicide. In a hypnotic state she broke down and cried her heart out, saying if only she had not gone out that weekend he might still be alive today. I encouraged her to cry as much as she needed, and when she stopped I explained to her that as she had not even been aware he intended to kill himself she could not possibly have been with him all the time. If he was going to do it she couldn't have stopped him anyway. I asked her if she loved her brother and she said 'Yes.' I asked her if her brother loved her and she again said 'Yes.' I then asked her to imagine that it was she who had killed herself and her brother was feeling very guilty about it. Would she want her brother who she loved to feel in any way responsible for her death when it was she who had killed herself? Would she want her brother to feel bad about the sister he loved or would she really like him to remember the love he had for her and feel good things about the one he loved. 'Oh Yes!' 'Then why don't you do feel good about your love for him?' She said she would try.

I again encouraged her to become the parent she never had. [**See my first book.**] I asked her if her own children were good children, and she replied 'Oh yes! very good.' I asked her did she not think that their being good children had something to do with her being a good mother? She agreed but didn't know how. Slowly over the next few visits I built up a better self image for Dorothy and got her to celebrate that good image often.

At one of her visits when she came into my consulting rooms she appeared very upset and she said she hated her husband, He was such a bully. I asked her why? She said reluctantly 'Oh he was on about wanting sex last night. While she was telling me this she burst into tears. After she had had a good cry and seemed to feel a little better about it all I asked her if we might explore her feeling about sex but she was adamant about not wanting to do anything about it. She wouldn't even talk anymore about it. So we again worked on building her self image. While we were doing this she again burst into tears saying she was not a very nice person. I asked her why? and she just said 'I don't know but I'm not nice.' I could get nowhere on this visit but I felt that something very important was surfacing and said to her that someday when she was strong enough to take it she would know what was really bothering her and she would be able to handle it. Doing psychotherapy is often like peeling an onion, you get one skin off, and again and again another is just underneath.

About four visits after this last one she was again very upset when she came into my rooms. She said she didn't want any more treatment and I asked her why? She burst into tears and slowly in fits and starts she told me about a dream she had had the previous night. Telling it was like drawing blood from a stone, in between crying and fits of anger. She said when she was ever so small her Father (Real Uncle] had taken her into his bed and he had made her do bad things to him. I thought Oh my God! here we go again. I had heard it too many times before to not believe it. I didn't want to believe it as I had some difficulty in knowing how anyone could do that to a child but here it was again. I asked her to tell me what he had done *[I knew what he had done but it was important for her to tell me so that I could help her to see it was not her fault.]*

She had great difficulty in telling me that her father had made her have oral sex with him. She said she could still taste his semen in her mouth, even now. She insisted she was dirty and a wicked person. She said she wondered if it was just a dream but she really knew it was not. *[She still didn't want to know about it or admit it to herself.]* After she had cried for some considerable time and was beginning to settle down I asked her how old did she think she was? She said about three. I asked her if a child of three knows what is right and wrong when its father tells it to do something. She said 'NO' I asked her if he encouraged her to do it and she said 'Yes'. Her Mother [Real Aunt] also encouraged her. *[I suppose it let her mother off the hook so that she didn't have to do it.]* It had happened very frequently and she was made to do even worse things, and her father told her not ever to tell anyone about it. She had seen a coffin at a funeral and her father had told her if she ever told anyone about it she would end up dead in a coffin. *[No wonder she had to suppress all knowledge of it.]* She was terrified of him but he gave her a reward of sweets after she had satisfied him each time. *[No wonder she was afraid of sex, and hated her husband when he complained of not getting any sex. He was symbolically her real uncle all over again who she hated.]*

Somehow her real parents had got to know about this and she remembered her real father coming to get her and having a blazing row with her 'uncle father' She said she thought he was going to kill him but she also thought somehow it was her fault. *[She had no chance, she had to repress it out of her mind.]*

It took me about six visits to get her over her guilt of this affair and eventually she told me she had told her husband. I knew then that she had forgiven herself. She said her husband was disbelieving at first but everything added up so he eventually came to believe it and was very sympathetic. A lot of things fell into place and made sense after these visits. She had met her aunt and uncle in a shop and confronted them with all her new-found information, but had been very scared. They tried to deny it but they were very embarrassed and obviously felt very guilty.

Dorothy wanted to prosecute them but I told her that it would be difficult to prove, especially as they would deny it, and as her mother and father were dead and they were hardly likely to have told anyone about it. It would be just her word against theirs. Also dirt sticks even if it is not your fault and her children may find out and be hurt by it. She agreed and we had a session where she told her aunt and uncle where to get off, in dream under hypnosis. I also told her she could really show them she was much better than them, by not letting what they had done to her, affect her now. She stopped being afraid of them.

We then worked on building her belonging to her husband and two lovely children and she became much happier, less afraid and she found she had a much better self image, and had many more options in her life.

I hope this case history shows you how damaging oral sex can be when a child is forced or tricked into indulging before it is old enough to appreciate what it is doing.

Oral sex is also very common among boys at boarding school. This also is often very damaging and can lead to homosexuality in later life. Often when two boys experiencing sex together are caught, the affair is hushed up at school, however, if a boy is caught with a girl in a boys' school all hell is let loose. This, **quite wrongly**, only goes to show the boys unconsciously that it is safer to be homosexual.

The treatment for all sexual problems of this kind has to be individual to suit the patient.

CHAPTER 5.

Anorexia Nervosa. The slimmers' disease and related disorders.

The terribly distressing, and often fatal, conditions of Anorexia Nervosa and Bulimia and vomiting, just like alcoholism or drug taking, are extremely difficult to treat because very often the patient doesn't want to get better, or refuses to accept the fact that they have a problem. So long as they refuse to co-operate, or are gravely under-weight, hypnosis is of little help, except perhaps to change their motivation in life. This can sometimes be done by explaining the marathon they swam to be here, and showing them that the purpose of life is to raise one's consciousness to a higher plane so that we become responsible for ourselves, otherwise we are just recycled to do it all over again. [**See my first book, 'How to Become the Parent You Never Had.'**]

Most anorexics are extremely unhappy with life, have a strong feeling of unworthiness and feel quite unlovable. They also have a strong feeling of being a failure. Because of these feelings they have a dread of growing up and having to take responsibilities. They become childlike in their behaviour, stubborn, aggressive, bad tempered and moody, and yet dependant, particularly on mother whom they seem to resent. They resent their dependence but refuse to grow up and take any responsibility for themselves, except for their over-skinny bodies, which they defend, unfortunately, sometimes to the death.

They have great difficulties in communicating with anyone and can't express their real feelings because they have shut off their real feelings. They quickly lose all their friends because their friends easily see how ill they really are, and become frustrated at attempting to help the anorexic,. who refuses all attempts of help, just to defend the modern pressures on women to be slim in order to be attractive. They see their skinny bodies as attractive, when everybody else is horrified. At least they **pretend**, even to themselves, that their skinny bodies are attractive, but when forced to look at photographs of themselves in swimming costumes they even try to deny it is them in the photograph.

In order to not eat they have to deny any feelings of hunger or emptiness and always have a false feeling of being full. Along with the fear of growing up, girl anorexics feel much better when they don't menstruate as this is a rejection of puberty and maturity. Most of them also reject sex for the same reason.

The incidence of anorexia nervosa is about twenty to one in young girls as opposed to males, generally between the age of eleven to thirty although it can occur in other ages. [See case histories.] Its onset is often at times of stress such as 'O' or 'A' level examinations, when there is tremendous pressure from unconsciously jealous parents, who didn't have the chance themselves to show their ability when they were young. Because of this the anorexic has an accompanied fear of failure which is always exaggerated by the parents' expectation.

Their behaviour is dominated by hectic physical exercise. They are always running up and down stairs, or moving at the double, to try to lose some more weight. Laxatives and purgatives are used all the time, once again in an attempt to control weight.

Let us try and look at how some of the concepts in their mental library may have been formed. Remember that perception is governed by learned concepts. Over-eating, smoking, drinking alcohol to excess, drug taking and anorexia may all have their roots in 'Cord' trauma.

During your nine months in the womb the umbilical cord acts as your friend and provider. It supplies you with all the food you need to grow, all the minerals, protein, fats, oxygen, hormones, and even antibodies that keep you healthy. In fact it is your total life support system. It is the main other thing besides yourself that moves in the womb, so it becomes your friend, companion, play-thing and first sex object. [It gives you pleasure to touch it and squeeze it, hence your first sex object] Scans of babies in the womb often show the baby playing with the cord.

It is my belief that anorexia nervosa is a learned behaviour that starts with cord trauma at the time of birth, or immediately afterwards at the cutting of the cord. This represents the first separation and loss we experience, when we have to rely on our external environment for sustenance and life. If the experience is traumatic, either by the cord getting in the way, or being occluded, with subsequent oxygen loss, in our struggle to get 'out'; or if the cord is cut too soon, before we have established a regular breathing pattern, once again with a 'cutting off' of the oxygen supply, the resultant feeling is one of being 'suffocated', 'killed, 'got rid of', 'shouldn't be here', and guilt for being here. These concepts learned at this traumatic time may remain as concepts affecting our perception of ourselves and our 'provider' for the rest of our life. They give rise to all subsequent love-hate relationships. How are we going to trust our 'mother', or 'provider', after that if those concepts remain unchanged.

If this first 'cord loss' experience is traumatic, the trauma experienced at any later, 'real', or 'imagined', abandonment by a parent, or parents, will be greatly exaggerated, and only go to reinforce the above learned concepts. If we 'come out' with those feelings we may ourselves cause the later rejection by having to refuse the one thing we want, which would make it alright for us, namely our parents' and/or any substitute, love. These feelings may form the basis of how we relate to the things that are important to us, including life itself. It may also lead to phobias of knives and being cut, and even needle phobias, [Needles going through the skin being partial cutting] in our later life. [Just another cutting of the cord.]

Little boys find a substitute cord in the penis and hold onto that. The bigger it is the more like the cord, hence the jealousy exhibited later, among men, in the size of the penis.

Many children have a 'fluffy' or blanket, or favourite cuddly toy which goes everywhere with them. The trauma expressed at the loss of such a 'comfort' far outweighs what should be the 'real' loss of such an object. I believe this shows the need and dependency to find a substitute, and the total unwillingness to give it up. I would go as far as to say that happiness, in later life, only comes to those individuals who have successfully replaced that need, with themselves, and become their own providers, and 'cord', totally responsible for themselves. [That is the very purpose of life itself. **See my first book.**]

Some children, and even adults, thumb suck as a substitute for 'cord' loss. Other people may substitute over-eating, smoking, drinking alcohol, or the taking of other drugs, hence the great resistance in giving up, what to them has become, a substitute 'cord' dependency. This giving up of a habit may be especially traumatic and any difficulty experienced in the giving up will be grossly exaggerated, if the first, and 'real' cord loss was traumatic.

Let us look at the correlation that exists between the behaviour of patients suffering from anorexia, and the concepts explained above which are formed from traumatic 'cord' loss; and how that relationship may shed some light on what otherwise appears to be totally unexplainable behaviour of the anorexic.

First of all, the most common time of onset of anorexia is at puberty, a time of uncertainty between childhood and adulthood. 'Cord loss trauma' occurs at the time of leaving the security of the womb for the uncertainty of the outside world. The anorexic doesn't want to get better because if they do they will have to grow up and mature and the final separation from mother will occur all over again with all the exaggeration of the trauma which occurred at that first separation. The fear that they will be 'cut off' in the world as they were at birth, with all the accompanied pain which that entails, ensures their resistance to growing up and forever losing any chance of being 'hooked up' to mother again. You get the typical 'psychological vampire' who goes round trying to 'plug in' an imagined cord into anybody who will provide succour, who will bleed you dry of any strength you may possess, only to spit you out and move on to their next victim. These people are not usually anorexic because they use other people as their defence against becoming anorexic.

The anorexic feels unworthy, unlovable and incomplete. 'Cord loss' makes the baby feel it has lost everything it needs, and therefore is incomplete and is being got 'rid of' so it is unlovable and unworthy. The anorexic fears failure, while the baby feels it cannot succeed without its 'cord'

The anorexic is stubborn, aggressive and yet dependent, at the same time resenting that dependency. The baby suffering 'cord loss' could easily be angry at the brutal cutting of the cord, wishing it was connected back, and therefore once again dependent, but resenting the need to have something that nearly killed it when it was removed.

The anorexic stubbornly rejects food by any means, even to the point of death, at the same time refusing the one thing they want which would help them, namely their mother's love. 'Cord trauma' may well control how we relate to the world and everything in it, including whether we live or die. If we can't trust our 'cord' at birth we may as well die later when we are about to lose all hope of ever regaining it. Then at least we won't need it any more.

There are twenty anorexic girls to every one boy, but if you remember my statement that little boys find a 'cord' substitute in their penis this fact is very understandable. After all, girls can't find that substitute except in men, possibly leading to the nymphomaniac behaviour of some women.

You may not like to accept these concepts, or the correlation between them and the behaviour of the anorexic. I don't claim them to be proven facts, but they do give an explanation of what otherwise would be unexplainable. If you can believe them and sell the idea to your anorexic patient, then you do have a logical treatment which works in quite a number of people and you will save some lives that otherwise would be lost. Psychotherapy is about telling a story which the patient will buy to get better. What better story can you tell than one that explains it all logically. If the anorexic is gravely underweight, I find it is always necessary for the patient to have gained some weight, if necessary by hospitalizing them first, before starting the treatment of building new concepts.

Valerie Stamp was a seventeen year old twin, about to take her 'A' levels. She was very anorexic and depressed. When she came for treatment she weighed six stone nine pounds, having just gained ten pounds, and was five feet six inches tall. She had a great fear of failing her exams, and thought her twin sister was much more successful than her. She had a very poor self image and thought she was a worthless person. She had thought about suicide [as well as starving herself to death, which she didn't considered was suicide] but was too scared to do anything. Her parents were both professional people and wanted her to achieve. She was a typical case of anorexia nervosa.

Valerie had a medium hypnotic capacity with a low resistance. She was not Organically Brain Dysfunctioned. I started building new concepts for Valerie by having her review the marathon she ran with her sister, while she was in a hypnotic state. Both she and her sister beat fifty-million other sperm to the two ovums waiting to be fertilized. [They were not identical twins] They both deserved to win, and they both did win that race to be here. When a race is a draw, neither is better than the other, and they both asked to be here. I had Valerie tell herself, in a hypnotic state, every two hours that she asked to be here, and she deserved to be here by winning a marathon. I had her then tell herself every two hours that she had just as much right as anybody else to be here, and especially just as much right as her sister to be here.

I had her review, in hypnotic dream, her birth when her sister got out first because that is how it was; but while she was getting out her cord became occluded and she became anoxic. [Suffering from a lack of oxygen.] She hated her sister for getting out first, and her cord for letting her down and nearly suffocating her but it was all accidental and no one deliberately did anything to make that happen. She was to go with her 'adult mind' to her 'birthing self' and tell and reassure her 'birthing self' that everything would be alright, and she would get 'out' safely; and nobody, especially her sister, or her 'cord', wanted to hurt her. They all wanted her to be safe and well, and loved her. She was to see herself 'out', safe and well and to see that no one was to blame and she could love them all, especially her 'new born self'. I repeated this a number of times on subsequent visits until new concepts about her sister, her 'cord' and herself were formed. In between visits she was to repeat the exercises in the above paragraph. It became obvious when her new concepts were being formed, when her feelings about her sister, her weight, and herself were slowly getting better.

On another visit I explained, to her in a hypnotic state, that both she and her sister were individuals in their own right. Each would do their own thing, each would be themselves, and not compare themselves with the other, as they were not in any way the same. Neither of them were in this world to live up to the expectations of anyone, or each other, just as others were not in this world to live up to either of their expectations. If either of them met on some common ground with anybody else then their relationships could grow, as they themselves would grow. [Some of you will recognise this as part of the Gestault Prayer.] I repeated this session on a number of occasions at different visits.

I had her create an image on a split screen of herself being unhappy, depressed, not eating, angry, resentful, jealous of her sister and feeling unworthy, on one side of the screen. While on the other side of the screen, she was to create an image of herself getting on with her own life, happy, maturing, being able to rely on herself, doing her best in her 'A' levels, regardless of what that was, eating normally and enjoying her food, knowing that she asked to be here, and knowing that she had every right both to be here, and at the same time to be herself. While she was doing this in a hypnotic state she was to choose which image she wanted to be. When she had chosen, she was to bring the one she wanted to be back from the screen, and integrate that image with herself by imagining what it would be like to be like that. She was instructed to leave the image she didn't want on the other side of the room. When she had integrated with the image she wanted ,she was to open her eyes and be that person. She was taught to do this exercise for herself every two hours for two minutes at a time until she only had one image on the screen. **The one she was, was the one she wanted to be.**

Valerie passed her 'A' levels and is getting on with her life and is now a steady seven stone ten pounds in weight.

The second case I would like to describe was also a typical case of anorexia nervosa. Gillian was twenty-six years old. She had been in and out of hospital a number of times before seeing me; each time a small weight gain had been achieved in hospital, but each time she came out, she again went down in weight. She had all the usual symptoms, behaviours, and poor self image of the typical anorexic. When she came to see me she had recently been in hospital and had been up to six stone five in weight, but had dropped to five stone nine pounds after she came out. She absolutely refused to go into hospital again, as she said she hated it, and complained that they were cruel to her in hospital. She was a medium capacity hypnotic subject with a medium to high resistance.

She was amazed at my explanation of why she should be like she was, and agreed with all the ideas, pointing out herself how each of her symptoms fitted the theory. Her mother said, 'She seems to trust and understand you, and this is the first time she has done that with any of her therapists'. She was very willing to talk to me about her condition, privately, when her mother was not present. [Showing a distrust in her Mother. I think she was afraid her mother would send her back into hospital, which in retrospect may have been the best thing.] However she continued to lose weight in spite of everything I tried to do with her. When she reached five stone four pounds she was very weak and I advised her mother to take her back into hospital. This case was before I realized how vitally important it is to get the patient's weight to as near to normal before you try to introduce new concepts. In the same circumstances now I would insist the patient is taken into hospital and treatment would not be started until a reasonable weight gain had been achieved.

She stopped coming to see me and her mother phoned me about six weeks later to tell me she had absolutely refused to go into hospital this time, and had died weighing only four stone five pounds. I hope this case shows how important it is to not try to treat anorexics who are very under weight until a satisfactory weight gain has been achieved, if necessarily in hospital. They seem to be unable to make the essential change in their concepts while they are gravely underweight.

The next case I would like to describe is not typical because the patient is a male. Henry was twenty-seven when his psychiatrist referred him to me to see if I could help him.

Dear Geoff,

Re: Dr. Henry Jasper Ph.D.

Anorexia-bulimia nervosa.

I would like you to see this young man who has requested hypnotherapy for the above condition. I enclose photostatic copies of my correspondence with his family physician, which I think covers everything relevant.

I would be grateful for anything you can do to help him.

Yours sincerely,

-----------—Consultant Psychiatrist.

Photocopy of letter to patient's Doctor in Birmingham where he works.

Dear Dr.-------

Re: Henry Jasper Ph.D.

Thank you for asking me to see this young man. He presents with a fairly typical anorexia—bulimia nervosa which, as you know, is a very uncommon condition in men though it does occur from time to time. He is a young man of twenty-seven, who admits that he has always been very weight conscious and something of a dieter. The more complex pattern of eating seems to date from 1979 when he was working for his Ph.D. He was then working all day on his thesis, became hungry, eat an excessively large meal at night, panic that he would as a consequence put on excessive weight and accordingly learn how to vomit this meal up, so that in the event he progressively lost weight. This seems to have set up a pattern for subsequent events in which he eats little or nothing during the day then 'bingo' eats at night followed by vomiting. His weight is now down to seven stones from a previous high of thirteen stones, and not surprisingly he complains of tiredness and lack of energy and stamina. I understand that he has been off work for the past two weeks. In addition to these symptoms he describes early waking, insomnia and frank depression of moods, so that one has this general associated picture of a depressive condition which is I think not uncommon in some patients with anorexia.

As you know, he is a man of twenty-seven who was born and brought up in the Morpeth area where his parents were both school teachers and continue to reside there. He has a younger sister who is currently a student at Sheffield. His family history is negative though his mother, he tells me, suffers from alopecia. He has always been highly strung and hypersensitive though his childhood was a happy one and he had a good school record, completing his time at the grammar school in Morpeth, and then going on to Newcastle University where he graduated in 1979 in physics. He remained as a postgraduate student and obtained his Ph.D. in 1982. As so often happens these days, this proved to be no high road to employment and for some six months he was unemployed. He took up his present post in Birmingham in 1983 and seems quite happy in his job, though he has become progressively concerned about his health. He is a single man who claims that he has always had plenty of friends both at home and at University. His previous health record appears to have been satisfactory. He asked me specifically whether this was a condition pointing to a homosexual potential on his part, since apparently this has been put to him, and declared with some emphasis that he has never been aware of any such propensities. Although it so happens that the only other male patient I have with Bulimia is indeed homosexual, I would not have thought that this was a necessary prerequisite and, however much one may speculate about underlying subconscious psychopathology and it remains to see what will emerge in this connection, I would not have thought that at this stage there is any reason to suppose that this is part of the problem.

What is nevertheless I think abundantly clear is that if we are to achieve anything positive with this young man, it will probably be necessary for him to have a period of inpatient hospital treatment and I was pleased to learn that he had in fact come to the same conclusion. I have therefore arranged to admit him, at the beginning of the week after next, which will give him an opportunity to attend to some practical matters which have to be dealt with before he can do this. I will naturally let you know what transpires.

With kind regards,

yours sincerely,

------------------------Consultant Psychiatrist.

Photocopy of letter sent to patient's doctor in his parents home town. Six weeks after the previous letter.

Dear Dr.-----------

Re. Henry Jasper Ph.D.

This young man, who is a Ph.D. physicist,normally living and working in Birmingham, tells me that you have always been his family doctor and as he is likely to be here abouts for the next two or three months I am writing to appraise you of the situation. He was in fact referred to me by his present family physician in Birmingham, on account of a rather unusual condition in a man, namely Anorexia-Bulimia Nervosa . I attach a copy of my letter to Dr,-----—about him which gives my general appraisal of the history and background. As you will see I then arranged to admit him to hospital, for a preliminary period of treatment and he has just been discharged therefrom to live for the present with his family.

My main concern during his period of inpatient treatment was to establish a more normal eating pattern and in particular regular small meals. There has been surprisingly little resistance on his part to this process. As a result of a period of under three weeks in hospital he has put on over a stone in weight and is certainly looking physically far fitter and better.

As is usual with anorexics he presented a general background of anxiety and depression and this has been very satisfactorily controlled by a combination of Chlorpromazine and Phenelzine which he is continuing to take in a dose of Chlorpromazine 25 mg t.d.s. and 50mg at night, and Phenelzine mg 15 t.d.s. However we have now moved on to the stage of looking perhaps a little more carefully at the background in an attempt to erect a meaningful psychopathology, this usually being rather more complex in the male. Just as with anorexic girls there is nearly always a rather difficult and complicated relationship between mother and daughter so in anorexic males the father/son relationship is often involved, with father seen as a somewhat authoritarian figure the son does not wish to challenge, except perhaps in rather subtle ways such as, in this young man's case, his academic attainment. It may well be of some significance that he first really began to run into trouble symptomatically not during his ordinary degree course but when he went on into his Ph.D. studies.

There are probably a number of other relevant factors. Firstly, as a small child he seems to have been rather obese and to some extent the butt of other children who teased him on that account. It is interesting too, I think, that at one time he had for some months a girlfriend who was a dietician, who used to talk a lot about food and diets, though interestingly at that time he had no particular problems in that regard himself. At this stage I have been primarily concerned with indicating to him the general type of psychopathological process which seems to be involved in these cases, namely on the one hand interest in and concern over one's body image and the implications this has for interpersonal relationships and on the other, eating as the incorporation of the external world into the self.

I have arranged to see him for a few psychotherapeutic sessions directed to the elucidation of some of these matters but he has also today expressed some interest in hypnotherapy and if after some further thought this is an avenue he would wish to explore, then I would be inclined to refer him to a Hypnotherapist colleague, whose expertise in that field is considerably greater than mine. For the present however he has certainly made some very major strides. He is obviously coping much more successfully from a general social point of view.

It is however I think desirable that he should continue with his medication for some little while yet and I would be most grateful if in the event that he comes down to the surgery, you would kindly prescribe for him.

With best wishes,

Yours sincerely,

--------------------Consultant Psychiatrist.

When I saw him I found he had a massive resistance to hypnosis and although he had a very good eye roll it was impossible to assess his hypnotic capacity. I asked him what he hoped I could help him to do with hypnosis. He gave me four areas he hoped we would work in.

1. He said he had an obsession with thinking about food. He just couldn't stop thinking about what he could eat next.
2. He wanted to stop thinking about being sick after he ate anything.
3. He wished he could get more fun out of life but didn't seem to know how to do that.

4. He hoped I could find a way to make him more confident in himself.

I talked to him about his mind being a little like a computer. It couldn't work until a programme was placed into it, just like a computer. Everything that had happened to him in his life that was significant had a memory somewhere in his mind, and those memories were like the programmes on discs that you put into a disc drive to start up a computer, only his memories were starting up his mind, even when those memories were long since forgotten consciously. Everything that he felt and did was controlled by the concepts that had been made from his memories. Those memories must be of traumatic times to make him have such bad feelings about himself. He was however proving that his concepts could make him feel things, even if those things were bad. I would like to explore his mind with him to see if we could find some good memories to load up his mind so that he could perceive with good memories. He knew a little about computers so he thought that was a very good idea. I made him another appointment to try that idea next time, giving him some time to think about it to see if his wishes would reduce his resistance.

The time delay worked perfectly. The next time he came into my consulting room his resistance was hardly noticeable. He went almost immediately into a medium trance state with a 'Speigel Eye Roll' induction and I took him through a dream re-run of the marathon he ran to be here. As I explained that he had beaten fifty-million other sperm to get conceived, it was possible to see the pleasure on his face at that thought. I went on to tell him, that as no-one was on this earth for any other reason, he had just as much right as anyone else to be here. Once again the pleasure showed on his face and he opened his eyes and said 'You know I had never thought of it that way'. I told him just to close his eyes and to go back to that re-run and while he was reviewing it I told him that every two hours of his waking day he was just to close his eyes by turning his eyes up to look at his forehead, then to close his lids and turn his mind inwards to review that marathon. While he was reviewing it he was to tell himself, 1. he asked to be here, 2. he beat fifty-million to win so he was clearly capable of winning and he had proved that, 3. because no one was here for any other reason he had just as much right as anyone to be here. 4. Because he won that marathon he could do anything he wanted, provided it was possible for most other human beings. When he had thought these things, taking no more than two minutes over it, he was to open his eyes and go about his business with those thoughts. By doing this exercise for two minutes about five times a day, in about twenty days those thoughts would be concepts by which he could perceive. After a little talking round the subject it was easy to see the excitement in his face so I made him another appointment in twenty days.

When he walked into my rooms you could see the change in his face. He was eager to start his next lesson. I repeated the last exercise and then told him that the cell he had created started to grow into two, then four, then eight, then sixteen and so on until there were thousands of cells which now took on the shape of a baby. I had him dissociate his mind from his body by imagining he was in a cinema watching a film of himself as a baby in the womb. He was to take his mind into the row behind his body so that it could watch his body in the row in front watching the film on the screen. I did this because I wanted to have him watch his birth and, because if my theories in this chapter were correct, there had to be some trauma in that film that I wanted him to see, but not feel.

Before I went on with the film we had an intermission in which I set up an ideo-motor finger response with him. I told him that the most common time in a person's life to learn negative behaviour was at the birth of that person. I then asked his unconscious mind if it would let us explore his unconscious concepts formed from the memories at birth to see if there was anything in those concepts that were responsible for his present difficulties that he had come to me to solve. His 'Yes' finger rose up into the air indicating its willingness to let us explore his memories of birth. I asked his mind 'Was there anything that was traumatic in his birth or immediately afterwards that was making him first of all gorge his food then reject it after he had eaten it?' His 'Yes' finger rose up once again. I asked 'Was it anything to do with his 'cord' that had provided him with food while he was in the womb?' His yes finger rose again. *[You may say these were leading questions, and that is why I got a 'Yes' answer. Who cares, if it helps and makes the patient have more options in their life about eating?]* I asked his unconscious mind if it would let his adult mind watch a film of his birth so that it could help his 'baby self' to get born without so much fear. His adult mind could then reassure his 'baby self' that it would end up alright because his adult mind was his 'baby self' in the future. His 'Yes' finger once again rose up.

We then returned to the film he was watching, from the row behind his body watching the film on the screen. It is my experience if you don't use dissociation in this instance when the patient sees the film, if it is traumatic, they become the film and relive the experience as a baby, and their adult mind gets lost in the feeling and is unable to help. He described the film as follows. 'The baby is really struggling but it is stuck and can't get out. The cord is getting in the way all the time and the baby wishes it would go away, it hates the cord for stopping it. He is very frightened about the whole birth, everything is unknown to him, and he is afraid he is going to die. At this point I asked his mind to go from the row behind his body to the screen and tell his 'birthing self' that it will be alright, he will not die, and no one wants to hurt him, it is just the way most babies are born. I said to him 'Tell your 'birthing self' that you know everything will be alright because you are that 'birthing self in the future. Help that baby to get born without fear with your adult mind, which understands what is happening. Then see that the baby is born and take it in your adult mind's arms and tell it you love it and will take care of it and keep it from harm until it grows up to be as old as you. Tell it that it needn't reject food anymore but will find a way of eating sensibly and enjoying reasonable amounts three times a day. When you see the baby is happy take it to your body back in the cinema and integrate your body and 'baby mind' and 'adult mind' all into one happy adult. When you are all one happy adult your 'Yes' finger will rise'. In a few seconds it rose up. I then said I would count to seven and when I got to seven Henry would open his eyes and be a fully integrated adult. I counted to seven and Henry opened his eyes and showed only amazement. *[I can almost see the doubters shaking their heads. Who cares, if it works and the patient has more options about eating? Perhaps Anorexia is so difficult to treat because it seems so impossible to understand.]* I then taught Henry how to help his 'baby self' to eat more sensibly; every two hours for two minutes at a time he was to turn his eyes up to look at his forehead, then close his eyes. Turn his mind inward and look at another screen divided down the middle. On one half of the screen he was to see himself eating everything in sight then making himself sick and ill afterwards. On the other half of the screen he was to see himself eating sensibly and feeling really good about how well and happy he looked. When he saw the two images he was to choose which one he wanted to be. Then bring back the image he wanted to be and open his eyes and be that one.

On his next visit he had said he was much better and realised it was all up to him to programme himself to become what he wanted. I only saw him for three more visits and taught him some more tricks to make positive concepts by which to live. He said he felt much better than he could ever remember and was now going back to work in Birmingham. I made him a tape of some of the exercises which he took with him. He phoned six months later to say he was still very well and enjoying life.

The last case I would like to describe is also not typical at all. Yvonne Wilks was referred to me by another patient I had successfully treated some time before. Yvonne was a fifty year old, seven stone, single lady living alone. She was suffering from anorexia, depression and agoraphobia. She went out to work but was afraid to travel on buses and hated crowds. A friend who worked in the same firm picked her up in his car, and took her both to, and from, work each day. She had great difficulty in doing her shopping, especially in food shops. Very often the mere sight of food would make her violently sick. She was very unhappy with her life feeling she always missed out. Her parents had died some years earlier and she now lived on her own. She was desperate for help and said the doctor had been unable to help her in any way. He only offered her anti-depressant tablets which she didn't like taking. Anyhow they didn't make any difference to her so she had stopped taking them. She was a very resistant hypnotic patient and her resistance made it impossible for me to tell what her capacity might have been.

I decided on the second visit that hypnosis wasn't the best method of treatment for Yvonne due to her resistance. I thought I would try some Reichian Hyperventilation to see if that would give me a clue as to what to do to help. After a few minutes of hyperventilation she began sobbing. I encouraged her to continue with her sobbing and while she was doing so I made a three minute loop tape of her crying. She insisted she didn't know what she was crying about, but felt generally very unhappy. I told her it was safe to cry here and encouraged her to do so until she could know what she was crying about. I told her her mind would only let her know what was upsetting her when it felt sure she could handle it with my help. Every time she stopped crying I played the loop tape of her crying back to her which started her off crying again. After only a few more minutes she began wailing and sobbing even harder. This time she said she knew what she was crying for. I asked her if she thought she could let me know what it was all about.

In fits and starts with sobbing in between she told me her mother and father hadn't been married, and when she was born, her father absolutely refused to accept that he was the father. He left, refusing to even speak with her, or her mother. She lived with her mother at her grandmothers house. Her mother had to go out to work to keep them as her grandfather was dead. If ever she saw her father in the street he would not speak to her. She sobbed even louder crying 'how could he do that?' She had been called 'the bastard' at school by the other children even before she knew what that meant. She felt so different from the other children, and never dared take anyone home to her grandmothers house, because they would see she had no father. She sobbed and cried and said she felt so guilty. She didn't deserve to be on this earth, and wished she was dead, but she was too scared to harm herself.

I asked her *'If you had a child would you expect your child to be responsible for anything that you did wrong? Just suppose you had a child and you killed someone, would you expect your child to have to go to prison because you killed someone?*

'Oh no!' she replied.

'Just suppose you had a child and you robbed a bank, would you expect your child to have to go to prison when you were caught?

'No it wouldn't be her fault that I had robbed a·bank.'

'That's right! it wouldn't be her fault would it?'

'No!' she answered.

'You are saying a child isn't responsible for what her mother does aren't you?'

'Yes! of course she isn't!'

'Are you responsible for what your mother did?'

'No of course I'm not, Oh!----[Silence]'

'How long a sentence have you served for your Mother and Father?'

'I suppose all my life.'

'Isn't it about time you let yourself out of prison then?'

'I suppose so.' She burst into tears again so I held her like a child and said,

'Go on it's safe to cry. Get rid of all that sorrow while I hold you.'

After a while she stopped crying and I gave her a paper handkerchief. We have boxes of them.

She said, 'Do you really think I wasn't guilty?'

'How could you be, were you there when your mother and father made love?'

'No of course not.'

'Then how could you be guilty? She smiled and I gently kissed her on the cheek. Actions are often better than words in that sort of situation.

I made her an appointment to return the next week. When she came in she looked tired and drawn and weepy. I placed the mattress on the floor and invited her to lie down. As soon as she lay down she began to weep. She said she hadn't been able to eat anything all week she felt much worse and asked if she should stop having therapy. Patients often feel worse for a little while before they get better, when you have opened

'Pandora's Box' and let them look inside. They also sometimes feel worse just before they are ready to give up a defence. This is because their unconscious mind is often afraid to give up a defence, even if it is a crippling one. There is a fear of 'what will I do when I can no longer have that defence, how will I cope with being well?'

I reassured her of the facts above and said *Why don't you try a few more sessions and see how you feel after that?* This is all she wanted, reassurance, she knew she had to go on. She began to cry again and said 'What a waste her life had been.' Every time she had got a boyfriend, when it began to get serious, she had to break it off. 'No one would want to have a girlfriend who was a bastard.' She cried even louder. I explained that when she was a child it was a stigma to be a bastard but now it is commonplace for parents not to be married, whether we approved of it or not. She had placed herself in 'prison' because of what her parents had done and it was time she came out into the world. She could only live now. It was no use crying over what was gone, that would only detract from any pleasure she may find now. She cried a little more as I held her hand, indicating that it was safe to cry, then she stopped and looked up. 'I suppose you are right' she said and sat up. We talked a lot more round this subject, about her affairs. How she had nursed her mother before she had died, how after her mother had died her father had come to her and said he was sorry he had not acknowledged her as his child. How she even nursed her father when he was dying. How now she was all alone. She cried some more. How there had been a man sometime ago, they had drinks together, but nothing else. He was married, he had said his wife didn't understand him, we've all heard it before. They met in a pub and had a few drinks on a few occasions, and talked about his children. I suppose he was safe as nothing serious could happen and she would never have to tell him she was a bastard. She cried again.

After a few sessions she said 'You know more about me than any other person in the world.' It's good to get it off your chest and have someone to confide in, we all perhaps need that. She began to feel much better. I gave her some new concepts to perceive her life with. She lost her fear of going out and her depression lifted. She began to take an interest in eating and found food was no longer sickmaking. She joined a country dance club and was enjoying herself. I saw her off and on for about two years and we parted with the understanding that she would come back if ever she had anymore doubts about living for 'Now.'

I hope these four cases have given you some insight into the very complex and confusing world of the anorexic, and shown you that they all need individual treatment. You can't win them all but you can try.

CHAPTER 6.

Verbal Diarrhoea. The constant talker.

We have all met the constant talker, the person who uses talking to cover up their inadequacy, or never stops talking, generally about themselves, to try to prove something about themselves. These are the people who constantly interrupt while you are talking, with something quite irrelevant to the flow of the conversation. Often it has nothing to do at all with what you were talking about in the first place. They often expect you to know what they have been thinking prior to their untimely and unwanted interruption, when in reality you haven't got a clue what the heck they are talking about. This is obvious when you become puzzled by what they say, as it seems to have no relevance to any prior information. Sometimes you may wonder if it is you who hasn't being paying attention, but fairly quickly you realise it isn't you. It is obvious they don't listen to what you are saying because they ignore any polite attempt to shut them up, and keep on with their irrelevant garble.

I am sure they don't even realise what a bore they really are, they are too intent in trying to prove something about themselves. I well remember an incident of this type when I was at a party. I was among a group of interesting people who were having a good discussion about something, when a person of the type described above joined the group. Within seconds of joining the group he was interrupting each speaker, eventually to take over the conversation almost all by himself. The people in the group, frustrated by not even being able to say anything and not understanding what on earth this fellow was trying to say, slowly began to drift away, one by one. I got so bored, and annoyed with this fellow, for breaking up what had been an enjoyable conversation, that after a while I could not restrain myself any longer. I interrupted him and said that I had been listening to him for the last ten minutes and had not understood a word he had been saying. Moreover I told him he had interrupted a very interesting conversation and had broken up the group because people were drifting away. I asked him to shut up and try to listen for a change and he might learn something. He gulped and choked and his eyes bulged, obviously he had not been aware of what he had done as he looked round and saw that most of the group had indeed broken up and drifted away. He shut up and soon drifted away himself. When he had gone a very good friend of his turned to me and said 'You know I have been dying to do that for a long time but have never dared. He is a nice fellow but such a bore. How on earth did you dare to say that to him?' I just said 'Quite easily. He obviously has an inferiority complex otherwise he wouldn't be talking as he does. He knows I don't, so he will take it from me.' I met the same 'bore' a number of weeks later at another party and when we came together he said to me 'How are you? The last time we met we had a little argument.' I just said 'Oh! no we didn't. I just told you the truth.' I then congratulated him on learning from our last conversation, which shut him up and stopped him in his tracks, and for once he just listened. We have become quite good friends now, and he is much better at listening, at least when he is in my company.

I remember another incident when another fellow was talking in the same group as myself and he, like the last 'bore', was going on and on about himself. He also was interrupting everybody and people began to drift away. I interrupted him and asked him how strong psychologically he thought he was. He said 'Fairly strong why?' I said 'I would like to tell you what I think of what you have been saying for the last quarter of an hour.' He said 'Go on then I would like to know.' I said 'I have never been so bored for a long time and I wish you would shut up and listen for a change, you may learn something.' He gulped and swallowed hard, but shut up and we continued with quite a good conversation. When he eventually left the group one of the other persons present said, 'I thought he was going to thump you.' I didn't feel he would as I was sure he, like the previous chap, felt inferior, and knew I didn't so he was prepared to take it from me. He probably wouldn't have taken it from someone who he didn't respect. I am sure that chap respects me more for being truthful. We still sometimes bump into each other and he is much better at listening now and seems just as friendly.

I am quite sure neither of the above people knew at the time they were being a bore and were unconsciously just defending their weak ego. Judging from their subsequent behaviour both had to adjust and at least they were not feeling weak and being a bore. They probably still felt weak, but if they learned to listen they would be liked a little more by other people, and may eventually get to like themselves a little more.

Another example of the constant talker is when the person has had to listen to a speaker at a meeting and in the question time, gets up to ask a question, but instead of asking a question, gives a long winded explanation of what he himself thinks, often on an unrelated or distant subject. Everybody else present thinks why doesn't he shut up. He never seems to realise what a bore he is because he does it all over again at the next meeting. He just seems to like to hear his own opinions. I suppose he somehow feels better for expressing them, but never realizes why everybody else pays no attention to him, and at the same time gets himself quite disliked. He often complains 'Why doesn't anybody like me, or listen to what I say?' If only he knew!

Audrey was an attractive young lady in her thirties who came to see me, by her own admission, because she talked too much. At least she realised it and wanted help. I asked her why she thought she should be like that. She said 'I am very neurotic and a bore and I just talk too much. I never say anything of importance but I just seem to prattle on.' People who suffer from 'verbal diarrhoea' take an age to describe their ailment in every minute detail. They don't, however, give you the real reason for their ailment. That is generally unknown to them consciously, or often very threatening to them. Audrey went on in great detail about her marriage being very good, but she said her parents were totally unable to give her any self confidence. I felt her marriage sounded too good to be true and made a mental note about that.

After some time it was obvious that she felt very inferior, so to shut her up for the time being I thought it would be a good idea to give her an ego boost. I did a capacity test and found she had a very high capacity with very little resistance. While she was in trance I asked her to access in her mind the marathon she had run to be here. I told her to tell herself that she asked to be here, then I went on to say that as she had won a marathon race she had just as much right to be here as anybody else. I watched her very closely as I said this and, as is very often the case in these people, a tear appeared in her closed eye as I said this last statement. I encouraged her to cry by telling her that it was O.K. to do that here, and it was safe to cry. She opened her eyes and said she had never been able to cry in front of anybody. Her parents had always told her to stop crying when she was little and now she couldn't cry when anybody was present. I told her just to close her eyes and have a good cry, it was O.K.

She burst into tears and had a good cry and said she felt so ashamed. I didn't think she was ashamed about crying because I had told her it was O.K. to do that so I said, *'You know most people have things that they don't like to tell anybody. Have you anything in your mind that you have never dared to tell?'* After a little more crying she said 'Yes I have.' I said *Would you like to tell me so that I can help you handle that?'* Again after a little more crying she said, 'Yes I would.' I remained silent for what seemed quite a long time, then she said, 'When I was about two I was so unhappy at home that I started to wet the bed. Actually I wet the bed until I was about eighteen. Oh! I feel so ashamed. I had to go to school in the mornings without having a bath. Everybody could smell that I had wet the bed. They used to tease me. I don't know how my parents could do that to me. They were useless as parents. They never showed me any love and I had to wear dirty smelly clothes. I feel so ashamed. I was terrified of the dark, I still am. I got psoriasis when I was six.' More tears. 'Then I got another skin disease. They took me to the doctor who gave me some cream to put on it but that smelled too. Then I got things in my hair and had to see the nurse at the clinic who gave me something to wash my hair with but that smelled too.' More tears. 'I always see my children are clean and have nice clothes to wear. I don't know how my parents could have done that to me. I know they were poor but you would think that they could at least have seen that I was clean and had clean clothes on.' She had just shown in this story that she had tried, unsuccessfully, at least three ways of getting attention. [*Three second line trauma defences.*] None of them seemed to work. Now she was using another in talking all the time and boring everybody with it. This was proving just as unsuccessful. Generally people suffering from 'verbal diarrhoea' are so busy using that behaviour as a defence, and attention seeking, that they don't see it is just another thing wrong with them that will result in rejection. It may get them attention initially, but it will be the wrong type of attention, and is doomed to end up as a counter-productive move ending up even further removed from homeostasis.

I explained all this to her and reminded her that she was a much better mother to her children than her parents had been. I asked her if she thought her children were responsible for the things she did. She said 'No.' So I asked her why she felt she was responsible for what her parents had done to her? She agreed she wasn't responsible so she shouldn't feel ashamed. I taught her to review the marathon she had run to be here, and had her tell herself that she asked to be here and she had just as much right as anybody else to be here. She was to tell herself that she had proved she could win by being here, and had already proved she was a better mother that her own mother so she needn't feel so ashamed. She was to do these exercises every two hours of her waking day for two minutes at a time until I saw her in a weeks' time.

When she came into my rooms, in a week's time, she was smiling and looked much more cheerful. She said she felt better than she could ever remember feeling in her whole life, and had been sticking up for herself to everybody. She mentioned she had been arguing with her husband because she had just realized that he also made her feel inferior. He preferred her to have to rely on him, that way he felt safer and more certain she would not leave him. It sounded like he needed some treatment. Whenever two people live together they find a balanced way to react together. If you change one, often, that balance is disturbed and you have to end up treating the other as well. Obviously her husband had been using her feelings of inferiority to cover up his own inadequacy, and now she felt stronger he resented it. I had thought the marriage sounded too good to be true the first time she had talked about it. She however insisted she wasn't going to let his weakness spoil her new-found confidence. She was amazed at how the exercises had changed her, and quite frankly so was I. I feel sure that being able to tell me what she had told me, the week before, about her childhood had also played a part in her recovery of self respect. She had said afterwards she had never ever told another living person about her childhood being so unhappy.

I taught her to use Speigel's split screen for her fear of the dark, and told her she could use it to change any behaviour she wanted. All she had to do was access the behaviour she had and then access the behaviour she would like in its place, and choose and tell her mind and be the new 'You'. I also taught her to use my 'scrap book' technique to review the things she did well, and to feel well and confident as her mental scrap book grew thicker.

She said she had stopped her incessant talking and that wasn't a problem any more.

She cancelled her next appointment saying she had never felt more confident in her life, nor better. She promised she would come back if she felt she needed to, but so far I have not seen her.

CHAPTER 7.

Nail biting and Thumb sucking, how to stop.

Another common defence used against feelings of inferiority or at times of stress is nail biting and thumb sucking. Like all the other forms of oral gratification described in this book the concepts used in nail biting and thumb sucking were formed at a very early stage in life. It is very common to see very young children in their prams sucking their thumbs or fingers. This form of comfort, I'm sure, is the child's attempt to have the breast back in their mouth. Very soon in life this form of comfort is relegated to the persons unconscious so that the hand or thumb automatically comes up to the mouth at those times of stress without the person even being conscious of doing that. Another common time to observe this dynamic form of comforting is at bed time. Many children suck their fingers or thumb at bed time, or substitute a 'softy' for their fingers. I am sure that some nail biters and thumb suckers learn this process as a 'cord loss' substitute while they are still in the womb. [See chapter 5. on 'cord loss'. Perhaps nail biting is a way of getting back at a cord trauma, after all both are destructive.]

I am sure that a 'softy' substitute, although it may prove difficult to get rid of, is easier to stop than persistent nail biting or thumb sucking in adults. I would also say that persistent nail biting and thumb sucking in adults is always a sign of a counteractive defence against a persistent high general tension level. There are always more efficient ways of reducing tension in adults than biting your nails or sucking your thumb.

In very young children, under three years of age, I'm sure

these forms of comfort are not in themselves harmful, other than they may form behaviours which may prove difficult to stop in later life. They may also indicate that the child needs more loving contact with it's parents, and I'm equally sure if it gets that loving contact the habit will be easier to control in later life. A 'softy' as a cord substitute is always easier to control than nail biting or thumb sucking in later life, so it may be useful to try to give such a substitute, if the child needs one and will accept one.

If, however, this learned habit continues into later childhood and then adult life it becomes counter-productive. The way the person is trying to relieve stress becomes the problem and causes stress, thus adding to the problem. The person with these regressive habits often has a very poor self image. It's almost as if the nail biter was punishing self for being such a bad or useless person. The masochistic pleasure they seem to get from mutilating their fingernails right down to the quick followed by contempt for self and embarrassment at what they have done, can clearly be seen as they then try to hide their fingers out of sight.

If, as the person gets older, they get more self confidence, or if they find a way to like themselves a little more by succeeding in whatever they are doing, providing they feel they are doing well, they will often just stop biting their nails, almost without noticing it. Many people who do well at something, however, don't themselves believe they are doing well. Everybody else thinks they are doing a marvellous job, but they still feel they are a failure. This is a result of a deep seated childhood feeling of being unlovable. These people, if they have learned to bite their nails, just go on, no matter how well they do, and get even more ashamed of themselves for mutilating their fingers.

I often find when I am helping someone to build a better self image for something else, they say 'I have even stopped biting my nails', when I didn't even know that was a problem, and I certainly hadn't done anything to help them in that direction. The 'spin off' in most psychological therapies, when they are successful, covers a multitude of sins, and in all sorts of ways the patient feels better. So the treatment of nail biting involves helping the patient to obtain a better self image, and to become more confident in themselves.

Specific treatments for nail biting are as shown in the following exercises.

EXERCISE 28.
Put yourself into a hypnotic state by turning your eyes up to look at your eyebrows, keeping your eyes turned up close your lids and at the same time 'let go'. Now turn your mind inwards to look at your mind and tell yourself the following five reasons for not biting your nails, one for each finger and thumb.

1. A little reason for a little finger. I will not bite my little finger because I'm hungry or tense because there is no food value in nails. In any case I spit the nail out so I don't need to get satisfaction by biting the nail so I won't.
2. Nails don't taste nice. They are covered with germs and bacteria that I pick up from all the surfaces that I touch so I won't bite my nails and I will be much healthier because I won't be putting germs and bacteria into my mouth.
3. When I was small I used to put my fingers into my mouth to comfort me, but grown ups don't do that. I will show myself and the world that I'm grown up, and have much better ways of reducing stress than biting my nails. In any case biting my nails makes me tense, afterwards, so I won't bite them any more.
4. Every time I put my hand out to shake someone by the hand I will feel proud of my hands, not ashamed because my nails will look good and manicured because I no longer bite my nails. I will never have to hide my hands again because I can be proud of them.
5. The last and big reason for not biting my nails. My hands are a part of my whole body and self. As I see my nails growing good and strong I will begin to like them like that, and as I do I will succeed in liking myself much more and feel much more mature and confident in myself.

I have just given myself five good reasons for not biting my nails so everytime my hands begin to move to my mouth to bite my nails I will become very aware that I don't do that anymore. Fairly quickly when both my conscious and unconscious mind know that, I will relegate that instruction to my unconscious and I will never even think of biting my nails again.

Now just open your eyes and enjoy your nails, looking good.

Do this exercise every two hours for two minutes at a time until you never think of biting your nails.

Milton Erickson describes another exercise for stopping biting your nails shown below in exercise 29.

EXERCISE 29.
In the hypnotic state tell your mind that you obviously get a relief of tension or something from biting your nails, but as you have five fingers on each hand you could leave one finger on each hand to grow big and long. Open your eyes and leave that finger to grow.

When that finger is beautifully manicured look and see how much more beautiful that one looks in comparison to the other four.

Again in the hypnotic state tell yourself that perhaps you could leave another finger to grow beautiful.

When you have two beautiful fingers tell yourself to have three, then four. When you have four beautiful fingers tell yourself it's a pity to spoil your hands with one finger so let them all grow beautiful.

EXERCISE 30.
Speigels' Split Screen.
In the hypnotic state create an image of yourself, on one side of a screen, with bitten fingernails, hiding your hands and looking ashamed and angry with yourself for being so immature. On the other side of the screen have an image of yourself with beautifully manicured nails, feeling pleased, proud and mature. Tell your mind which 'You' you want to be, and bring that 'You' back from the screen, leaving the 'You' you don't want on the other side of the room. Open

your eyes and be that 'You'.

Do this exercise every two hours for two minutes at a time until your nails are grown, and beautiful.

Thumb sucking is another form of comfort, like smoking or nail biting, that we learn as a substitute for the nipple, to give us relief from tension, anxiety, loneliness or stress. Teenage or adult thumb suckers generally are exhibiting an arrest in the normal maturity process. If and when they eventually mature they nearly always stop sucking their thumb without any difficulty. One of the problems of thumb sucking is that it tends to cause a disfigurement of the teeth. Either it results in the upper teeth being very forward and 'bucked' or there is an anterior open bite, which means that when the back teeth are closed the front teeth don't meet and the space between the front upper and lower teeth is most unsightly. Anterior open bites are also very difficult to correct with braces later on.

Small children are often brought into the Dental consulting room by mother,or father, who say [If it's father he generally says 'Mother' says] he, [or she, the child. Why father has to blame mother I don't know] has to stop sucking his thumb. Tell him he has to stop or he will make his teeth crooked.'

I find that most children, by the time they are dragged into the dentists', are sick of being told what to do, and what not to do. They have built up a resistance to being told what to do, by adults. It just goes in one ear and out the other, so the dentist is just another adult telling him what to do, and often the child doesn't even like the dentist, so why should he take any notice of him. This is another case of the parents passing the buck. Their excuse is the child takes no notice of me, he may listen to you. They have just lost the ability to communicate with their children.

If the above paragraph is correct you have very little chance of winning by telling little 'Johnny' to stop sucking his thumb or his teeth will be crooked. Little 'Johnny' doesn't care if his teeth are crooked he just wants to be left alone to suck his thumb.

When little 'Johnny' is not looking closely at you, look at his hands to see if one thumb is cleaner than the other. If it is you can bet that is the one he sucks. Tell little 'Johnny' you can see he likes sucking this thumb, pointing to the clean one. If he hasn't seen you looking at his hands little 'Johnny' often doesn't know how you know which one he sucks but he sees you are right so he listens to find out how you knew. Then you say 'I bet you like sucking your thumb, it's a great comfort, all children like to suck their thumb.' You have just said it's alright to suck his thumb. You must be SOME adult. You are the first one to tell me I'm alright, what are you going to say next? This of course is where the punch line comes. 'Yes all children like sucking their thumb, big boys don't. Bye-bye see you in four months time.'

Pretty soon little 'Johnny' gets to thinking what you said because you are the first adult who understands him. But little 'Johnny wants to be a big boy, all little boys do. So he says, 'I won't suck my thumb and then I'll be a big boy.' Nobody told him, he thought of it all by himself. He is much more likely to take notice if he thought of it himself.

If that doesn't work, the next time little 'Johnny comes in, one of his thumbs is still cleaner than the other, so you ask him if he has any brothers or sisters. If he says 'Yes', ask him if he has to share thing with them, or anybody else. If 'Yes' you then say 'You know, I know you like sucking your thumb but it's not really fair. You only suck one thumb and you have eight other fingers and another thumb.' Thumb suckers have a preferred thumb, they generally only suck the preferred one. 'I want you to give all the other eight fingers and your other thumb a suck as well, so they don't feel left out.' Then tell mother or father to see all eight fingers and both thumbs get the same time being sucked. Pretty soon little 'Johnny' gets sick of having no time left for himself, for sucking all his fingers and two thumbs. Anyhow the others aren't so nice to suck, so if I have to be fair I will suck none. I find as much success doing that as any other technique with small children. It is important to get the parents co-operation with the above two techniques. Often the child is getting back, or getting attention from the parent by sucking his thumb. The child sees his parents are annoyed and they are forever telling him to stop [Bad attention is better than no attention.] You must tell both of his parents to say nothing to little 'Johnny' about sucking his thumb, let him decide. If the second technique is necessary all his parents are to do is to insist he gives all the other fingers a go. Then little 'Johnny' can stop to get back at his parents again because they are telling him to suck his fingers. They had already lost the ability to tell 'Johnny' to do anything or they wouldn't be bringing him to see you in the first place.

If thumb sucking is continued when the person is a teenager or adult it is no use using the above two techniques. An interesting case occurred when I was helping a fifteen year old girl stop sucking her thumb. When I questioned her by herself [She indicated she didn't want her mother to be with her when she was having treatment, which was the first indication they don't get on. If they did she would normally have wanted her mother there for moral support.] She made it plain she didn't want to grow up and was using sucking her thumb as an attempt to stay dependent and childlike. She didn't say this in as many words but it was obvious that this is what she was doing, by what she was saying.

In trance I told her that it was inevitable that one day would be followed by another. That being the case it was inevitable that we would get one day older each day. The purpose of life itself was to get one day wiser each day. The longer we put off that purpose the more difficult it would be to make up for lost time. If we didn't make it up, we would just be recycled to do it all over again. So it is imperative that we get one day more able to be aware of things as they really are now, more able to cope with difficulties in a real manner, no longer staying childlike or regressing to childish habits. I asked her to remind herself that she asked to be here; that she won a marathon to be here and proved she could make it herself. I then had her do exercise 31 below, every two hours until she had no desire to suck her thumb.

EXERCISE 31.
Speigels' Split Screen.
In a hypnotic state make an image on one side of a screen of yourself sucking your thumb. See how childish you look,

and because you are acting childishly see how unhappy you really are. See how sucking your thumb is even making your life worse because no one takes you seriously.

On the other side of the screen see yourself coping with life in a much more mature way without sucking your thumb. See how much more seriously other people take you now that you don't just behave childishly. See how much happier you are, now that you are getting wiser every day. Now chose which 'You' you want to be, and tell your mind. Bring back from the screen the 'You' you want and open your eyes and be that 'You'.

CHAPTER 8.

Grinding your teeth away, and allied behaviour.

Many people grind their teeth as a counter productive defence against tension. It is counter productive because it doesn't reduce tension but generally increases it. Bruxism, as teeth grinding is called in the dental profession, is reasonably common, especially at night when the patient is asleep. Sufferers from bruxism wake up in the morning with their jaws and teeth aching. On inspection of their mouth it is possible to see flattened ground cusps in many of their teeth. If you think about somebody being really anxious or afraid you can picture them with their heads withdrawn into their necks, their shoulders up and their teeth tightly clenched. Perhaps this is the way a baby comes through the pelvic arch, apart from the clenched teeth, as the birthing baby doesn't have any teeth usually. They may, however, clench their jaws. If you ask patients who grind their teeth at night about the state of their pillow in the morning they will often say that the pillow is all scrunched up, showing that it wasn't only their teeth that were tense during the night.

The masseter muscles which are used in tooth grinding are commonly used to repress tension. This can often be demonstrated by pressing your thumbs on those muscles on either side of the jaws. Often they will be very painful and the patient will flinch and cry out when this is done. The treatment most commonly given for bruxism is to make a slipper denture which fits over the teeth to keep the jaws slightly open. This however is not always successful in stopping the grinding.

Cynthia was referred to me from the dental hospital as a

case of bruxism which was not responding to a slipper denture treatment. She had quite marked erosion of her teeth in all four quadrants of her mouth. She complained of severe jaw pain particularly on waking, and had been told by her parents that she had been grinding her teeth all night and every night. They could hear her doing this when she was asleep. The slipper denture which the hospital had made her was being ground into her gums so that her gums were sore and ulcerated.

Cynthia was a twenty-six years old solicitor's secretary, doing some part time nursing. She displayed signs of a high general tension level and anxiety, and had been having migraine attacks about twice a week for the previous three years. She was afraid of travelling in cars or buses, particularly in buses as she had been travelling in a bus, five years prior to seeking treatment from me, when it had crashed. She had not been seriously hurt, only shaken and had suffered from shock. The grinding of her teeth had started about a month after her involvement in that crash. She had difficulty in getting to sleep at nights and was taking sleeping pills and some other pills for the migraine attacks, which she had obtained from her doctor.

She had a high hypnotic capacity with very low resistance, which meant that I should be able to help her quite considerably without too much difficulty. I induced a trance state and gave her some specific suggestions on relaxing when she went to bed, and on being able to get to sleep easily when ready for sleep. I taught her to use my scrap book technique to feel more confident and showed her how to use Calvert Stein's clenched fist technique to reduce tension. These two techniques are described in exercises 32 and 33 at the end of this chapter.

After her second visit she reported she had had no more migraine attacks, and felt much more relaxed. I had not given her any suggestions about migraine and the cessation of attacks came purely from a 'spin off' effect of being more generally relaxed. She was sleeping much better and had not needed any sleeping pills or anything for her migraine following her second visit. She was, however, still grinding her teeth by the time the third visit came round.

I decided to try some ideo-motor finger responses to see if there were any dynamic forces making her grind her teeth. Her finger rose when I asked her 'Had the bus crash anything to do with the grinding of her teeth?' I then had her relive the crash in hypnotic dream, with the safeguard that she would not experience anything that she was not strong enough to feel at this moment in time. She remembered that when the bus had crashed she had been flung onto the seat in front of her. She had been winded and wanted to scream but couldn't get her breath to do so. She was very frightened and showed a lot of negative emotion by crying and moaning during the reliving of that scene. She said there was a loud crash of breaking glass so I told her if she wanted to scream to do so now. She let out a piercing yell filling the room with moans and crying. When she calmed down, in her own time, I reminded her that that crash was over five years ago and she didn't need to feel it any more. Afterwards she said she felt 'lighter' as if a burden had been lifted.

On her next visit she reported that she had stopped grinding her teeth, the pain had gone and she felt generally much better. She had been to the dental hospital for her checkup and the consultant had said she was like a different person, and he couldn't believe such a change could take place in a person in such a short time without seeing it for himself. She had been attending the hospital regularly for four years without much improvement before having this hypnotic treatment. He suggested she should continue a little longer with the hypnosis. On her next visit with me I once again regressed her to the bus crash and once again she released some more negative emotion, but not as much as the first time, which indicated that she was getting over it. Like a horror movie the more you see it the less frightening it becomes.

On her next visit she reported she had had no migraine since her second visit, her grinding had stopped after her first regression to the bus crash, she was sleeping much better without pills and she was no longer frightened of travelling on buses. She also reported she had just started to take driving lessons for herself. She said she had never even dared to think about driving before her treatment. Eight weeks later she came for her next treatment and she was very well and about to take her driving test, and reported never feeling so happy. Everybody was commenting on how well and confident she looked.

I saw her a year and a half later and she had had a little trouble at home over nothing special. She was standing up for herself for something which resulted in her having an argument with her mother who had told her if she was going to be like that she could leave home. She had started to grind her teeth a little but it was not as bad as before. I set up an ideo-motor finger response and asked if there was any more dynamic energy tied up with the bus crash and I got a very slow and weak response. I asked her unconscious mind through her finger response if there was another time which created a dynamic force which was now responsible for her grinding, and this time there was an instant and powerful response. I asked her unconscious mind if she was strong enough to know what had caused this other dynamic force, and we again got a 'Yes' answer.

I told her that when I said the word hurt and pain she would begin to feel hurt and pain, and the hurt would take her back to the time when the pain had been first felt. I said *'Hurt, Pain. Feel what is causing the hurt.'* She began crying. I encouraged her to cry at the same time asking her unconscious mind to let her know what was making her cry. She began whispering 'No mummy. No!' I asked her what was happening and she said 'Mummy and Daddy are arguing. They tell me to go to my room, but I have just gone out of the room and I am hiding behind the door. I'll get wrong if they hear me here. Mummy is shouting at daddy 'You wish I was dead, don't you' Daddy doesn't say anything and now Mummy is running outside and she slams the front door. She is going to throw herself under a bus and die I know she is. They were talking about a man who threw himself under a bus and died just yesterday. I want to shout out but I'm too frightened. They will hit me if they think I have been listening.' *'What are you doing now?'* I asked her.

I am going up to my room. I'm very frightened and I just cry
myself to sleep.'
'When you wake up where is Mummy?'
'She is downstairs in the lounge.'
'She hasn't killed herself, then?'
'No she hasn't thrown herself under a bus after all.'

Now we can perhaps see the connections. When Cynthia
was only three she thought her mother was going to throw
herself under a bus because she had overheard someone
talking about that the day before. She had wanted to cry out
but hadn't been able to because she was too scared. She had
gone to sleep still frightened and probably learned to grind
her teeth then when she was asleep. When Cynthia was 21
she was involved in a bus crash and wanted to cry out but
had been unable to because at the time she had been winded.
She was very scared at both times. The second time she had
started to grind her teeth in her sleep, a few weeks later. We
got rid of that dynamic force when we had her review the
crash in hypnotic dream. When her mother had told her she
would have to leave home after an argument she began to
grind her teeth all over again. The argument with her mother
was the trigger this time.

Cynthia stopped grinding her teeth almost immediately
following this last session, after she had been able to have a
good shout at her mother, and again release more tension
around that incident. I reminded her that the incident was
over and she need never feel tense about it again. She has
been well to my knowledge ever since.

Another patient Jennifer was referred to me from the
dental hospital with trismus of her mandible. This is an
involuntary cramp in the muscles of the jaw causing pain,
and an inability to open her jaw more than a few millimetres.
She had been having heat treatment to her muscles with an
infra red lamp, and they had tried a slipper denture, but she
got no relief from the cramp. She had been attending the
hospital for about six months when I saw her.

Jennifer was twenty-nine years old, a social worker,
married with no children. She was happily married and there
was no psychological history either in herself or her family.

Her father had died when she was fairly young, and her mother was not demonstrative with her feelings. Jennifer could think of no reason why she should be like this. She claimed nothing, other than her trismus, was bothering her and she had everything going for her. She had just woken up one day to find she couldn't open her mouth and it had gone on like that for the past six months, and shortly after it started her jaw had become painful.

I hypnotised her and found she had a very high hypnotic capacity. When I did 'Speigel's' capacity test with her hand on top of her shoulder I suggested her shoulder may want to keep her hand there, and she found she couldn't move her hand away from her shoulder. While in trance I suggested that in a few moments time I would count to seven and she would wake out of trance but her shoulder may still want to keep her hand there. The harder she tried to remove her hand the more her shoulder may want to keep it there even although she was no longer in trance. I counted to seven. She opened her eyes and I asked her if she had any more control in either of her arms over the other. She moved the arm not on her shoulder but when she came to move the arm with her hand on her shoulder she found, much to her amazement, that she had no control over it at all, and couldn't move it from her shoulder. I told her that for some reason she was doing to her jaw exactly what I had just done to her arm. She looked at me with some disbelief, so I said *'go on then it's your arm move it.'*
She couldn't move it even an inch off her shoulder.
So I said *'it's your jaw go on move it'* and she could only open it about three millimetres. *'So what is the difference?'*
She shook her head, there seems to be no difference.'
'No there isn't any, is there?'
'No!'
'O.K. I'll do a deal with you. If your unconscious mind will let you move your jaw I will give you full control of your arm back. Is That O.K.?'
She nodded her head approvingly.
I rehypnotised her and said *'when I snap my fingers you will wake from trance and find you have full control of both your hand,*

arm and jaw.' I snapped my fingers and she opened her eyes,
dropped her arm and said
'what do you want me to say?'
I said nothing and only watched her. She opened her mouth
very wide and rubbed her jaw and said 'My God! what am I
going to tell them at the dental hospital?'
I said *'just what has happened.'*
She said 'they will never believe me, I don't even believe it
myself.' I made her an appointment for two weeks time and
when she came in I didn't have to ask her anything. She was
talking away and opening her jaw easily. She said all the pain
had gone and she couldn't believe it. I taught her to relax her
whole body including her jaw and to my knowledge she has
had no more trouble. I'm sure she would come back if she
had. Sometimes a few hypnotic words can save a lot of pain
and trouble.

The last case I would like to describe in this chapter is
Jonathan, a friend of another patient of mine Phillip [who I
described in my first book under the heading of Miracles
happen only rarely in chapter 7.] Jonathan had been
recommended to come by his friend Phillip. Jonathan was
suffering from a gagging reflex whenever he ate food. He
found meat was the worst, he was sick every time he tried to
eat meat, and lots of other food made him retch. He
obviously was eating some things because he was not under
weight. His doctor had told him he could see no reason for
his gagging and he would just have to eat fish which he
didn't gag on. This gagging reflex had started after he had
had a fall in his garage. He had been up a ladder and was
leaning over and the ladder and he, with it, toppled over. He
hurt his back and had seen lots of specialists who had told
him, once you have a bad back it will always give bother. He
had become resigned to having a bad back and was walking
with two walking sticks.

He had had all sorts of medical examinations by specialists
for his throat and nothing could be found to cause his
gagging. They all said he had a hysterical gagging reflex and
as fish didn't affect him he should eat fish. The only trouble
was he didn't particularly like fish. He also had a small partial

denture which he didn't wear because that also made him gag. He had no other relevant medical history. He was happily married, had a good job and there seemed to be no psychological reason for having a hysterical throat. He said he was convinced that hypnosis would cure him because he had seen such a remarkable change in his friend Phillip after he had hypnosis.

I did a capacity test for Jonathan but it was difficult to be certain what his capacity was because he had a giant size resistance to being hypnotised. I can only assume in retrospect that his hypnotic capacity was higher than I could assess on the initial attempt. I thought that it was in the lower medium capacity level but in retrospect, judging from results, I would say that it was at least higher medium to high. His utter belief may have helped, along with his motivation to be cured.

Having done a capacity test and found his resistance to be massive, I reassured Jonathan that he would feel no different when he was hypnotised, but to go along with what I was doing with him. I did a Speigel's eye roll induction which by itself indicated a high capacity, and reframed his gagging reflex as described in exercise 34 at the end of this chapter. I also had him do a Speigel's split screen for his gagging and his back pain, as in exercise 35. I asked him to do the split screen exercise for two minutes every two hours during his waking day. Because of his resistance I made him an appointment for four weeks time, giving him enough time to try to work with himself. I felt he was less likely to resist himself, and with his belief and motivation it may just work.

Miracles sometimes happen twice. He came back in four weeks time with a smile all over his face. I didn't have to ask him if he was better, it was obvious. I only needed to know how much better he was. He said 'My back has been marvellous, I haven't used my walking sticks for over two weeks now. I've timed myself walking to the club from my home, it used to take me well over half an hour. Now I can do it in a quarter of an hour. Today I cut the hedge myself, I haven't done that for years. I may have over done it a little. I had a short rest on my bed afterwards, and see I'm walking alright now.' He got up and walked across the room. 'I'm eating well with no gagging reflex. I'm even wearing my denture.

I hypnotised him again, and this time there was no resistance. He went into what I would assess as a deep trance. I taught him some more simple exercises to help himself with a few precautions about not doing too much to strain his back. I have not seen him since but he promised to return if ever he needed to.

EXERCISE 32.

Geoff Graham's Scrap Book technique for confidence.

In the Hypnotic state imagine a beautiful book on your knee with your name on the front. This is a scrap book of all the things you do well. On the first page picture yourself sitting in the chair that you are actually sitting in, with your eyes closed, in a deep hypnotic state. To anyone else looking at that picture, they may think you are asleep, but you know you are not asleep. You know your mind is so attentive to whatever you tell it, that you will feel the emotions connected with what you are telling it, just as if the thing you are telling yourself were happening to you now. Now look at that picture and feel how comfortable you are now.

Now look at how well you have learned to go into the hypnotic state, and feel that now. Feel how successful you are at entering the hypnotic state, and hang on to that success. Use that feeling of success to feel the success you are at being a very good solicitor's secretary. Picture that in your scrap book. [In this place put anything you do well, no matter how small a thing that may be, and feel how good it is to do something well.] Hold on to that good feeling, and imagine how good it would be to be wide awake with that good feeling.

Before you open your eyes look at another picture in your scrap book of a time when you felt marvellously relaxed and happy. Hold on to that relaxed feeling, hold on to that happy feeling. Now imagine how good it would be to be wide awake with that relaxed, happy and successful feeling. Open your eyes and be wide awake with that relaxed, happy, and successful feeling and do whatever you are doing, with those good feelings. When you do, you will probably do, whatever you are doing much better, with those good feelings. Put those things you do better in your scrap book the next time you look at it, and as your scrap book grows thicker and thicker with things you do well you can't help becoming more confident in everything that you are doing. [This is taking the well accepted concept of free floating anxiety, and working it in reverse by taking a good event and using the positive emotion from that to feel good now. With free floating anxiety you are taking a negative event and using the bad emotion to feel bad now.]

Repeat looking at your mental scrap book for two minutes at a time, every two hours, until you feel very well, and repeat if you lose that good feeling.

EXERCISE 33.
Calvert Stein's clenched fist for tension reduction.

When you are in a hypnotic state think about something really good and strong, and imagine that you could hold that really good and strong thing in your dominant hand. Make a fist in your dominant hand and squeeze that good and strong thing until you feel as if the strength and goodness was going into your hand and up your arm and into your body. Hold on to that feeling.

Now think about any tension you can feel in your body and realize how negative that tension is. Make a fist in your non-dominant hand and imagine as you grip your non-dominant hand that all the tension is being drawn down into your non-dominant fist. Feel that tension being drawn down into your non-dominant fist and when it is all in your fist, hold on tight to it and don't let it back into your body.

While you are holding, tightly, all the negative tension in your body in your non-dominant fist, think about that really good and strong thing again in your dominant fist. Squeeze up your dominant fist and feel all that good strength moving up your dominant arm into your body, across your shoulders and down your non-dominant arm to your clenched fist. When all that good strong feeling reaches your non-dominant fist just open your non-dominant hand and let all the negative tension be pushed out by that good strong feeling. When all the negative tension has been pushed out of your fist by your good strong feeling onto the floor just open your dominant hand and feel relaxed, good and strong all over. Remember your dominant hand is always stronger than your non-dominant hand.

Repeat this exercise for two minutes at a time three or four times a day until you feel good and strong all the time and repeat if the feeling leaves you.

EXERCISE 34.

In the Hypnotic state contact that part of your mind that makes you gag on food. [You can substitute here, for gagging, any other behaviour you may want to rid yourself of.] Thank that part of your mind for trying to help you by making you gag. Then respectfully remind it that unfortunately the way it is trying to help you, by making you gag, has become the problem. While that part is listening, paying attention and wanting to help you, contact another part of your mind that weighs up all the pro's and con's of everything you do. Thank that part for helping you and ask both parts to get together in your unconscious mind, to debate and discuss ways that the first part could continue to help you without having to make you gag.

When they have discussed and agreed on a few ways in which the first part could help you, without having to make you gag, thank them both. Ask the first part to try some of these new ways of helping you until you find a better way of behaving. You will not be consciously aware of how they are going to help you because you asked them, deliberately, to discuss and debate the ways in your unconscious mind. This is done this way because if you know how the part is going to help you, you may try too hard to make it work which may spoil it and stop it from working. Sometimes the harder you try to do something the more impossible it becomes to do it. If you don't know, consciously, you will just do it, and may be pleasantly surprised. If you are not, repeat the exercise until you are.

EXERCISE 35.
Speigel's split screen.

In the hypnotic state create an image of a screen, divided down the middle, on the other side of the room. On one side of the screen, create an image of yourself gagging on your food, and always being aware and focusing your attention on the pain in your back.

On the other side of the screen create an image of yourself eating and enjoying all your food. Also see yourself being much more interested in what you are doing and what is going on around you so that you hardly notice your back.

Tell your mind which 'You' you want to be, and bring back from the screen the 'You' you want to be, leaving the 'You' you don't want on the other side of the room. Integrate the 'You' you want by feeling what it would be like to be that 'You' and open your eyes and be that 'You'.

PART 2.

Defending our mouth to the point where the defence becomes the problem.

Why do we do it?   Can we stop?

CHAPTER 9.

The dental phobic.

In Part One of this book I have shown how we all use our mouths as a defence against all sorts of psychological weaknesses. We use it to not feel lonely, to reduce stress, to reduce tension, to make us feel less psychologically empty inside, to feel less guilty, to win and be good, to reward ourselves and to make us strong. We also use our mouths to belong, to be grown up and look bigger, to be more mature or even 'macho', to cope with the difficulties in life, to concentrate, and to opt out by not feeling unpleasant feelings.

We use our mouths as an important part of sexual behaviour, as in kissing and oral sex. Then again, we use the mouth as an expression of anger, as in shouting, yelling or even biting. The mouth is an important part of communication, both verbally as in talking, and non-verbally as in smiling or grimacing, and even as a defence against interiority in talking all the time. We also use it as a defence by sucking the thumb or biting our nails. We even use it to repress painful experiences from the past or present as in alcoholism or drug taking.

Then we use the mouth to eat and chew our food, to taste food. We sing, laugh and express many emotions with our mouths. Because of all these different and varied functions performed by our mouths we have a very complex and extensive nerve supply, making the mouth an extremely sensitive organ of the body. Is it any wonder we defend it, sometimes to our detriment?

The dental phobic is one who does just that. They defend their mouths to such an extent that they will not have

necessary dental treatment to maintain good all round
health. There are as many reasons for being a dental phobic
as there are phobics and I would like to describe just a few
here. Perhaps one of the most interesting facts I have
discovered in treating thousands of phobics is that I have yet
to meet a very bad dental phobic who can cuddle both of their
parents affectionately. You might say what on earth has
cuddling both parents got to do with being a dental phobic?
At first sight it may seem nothing, but why can't really bad
phobics do what, after all, should be a simple thing? It is my
belief that the really bad phobics are so full of 'primal pain'
that they daren't face any other potentially painful experience. They have been so hurt in the past by their parents,
[*That's why they can't cuddle them.*] that to face another
person, namely the dentist, who might hurt them, is just too
much of a risk, which they are not prepared to take.

They seem to be almost proud to admit to being a coward
about dental treatment. They say in an almost boastful way,
'When it comes to dentistry I am yellow right down my
back,' or something like that. Why should they be proud to
admit to being a coward about anything? I believe they do it
to cover their unconscious guilt of not having their necessary
dental treatment. The unconscious argument goes-'I would
have my treatment if I wasn't so afraid, but I can't help being
afraid. I will admit to being afraid then I won't need to feel so
guilty about not having my treatment. Having the treatment
would be even worse than admitting to being afraid.' I can
see no other reason for admitting to being a coward so
readily.

They also use the 'blame game' to relieve their cowardice,
by blaming something else for their fear. They will tell you,
'It's the drill, or the sound of the drill, or the needle,'' or
anything but themselves to blame for their fear. This relieves
the guilt of being afraid, but it makes it much harder to help
them have their dental treatment. If they are using 'projection' as a defence, which is what blaming the drill, sound
of the drill or needle is, then to make their treatment easier
the dentist will have to remove the drill, sound of the drill or
the needle. It may, however, be necessary to use the drill,

sound of the drill or the needle, and if this is the case the patient is almost doomed to experience both pain and fear which only confirms that they were right in the first place to be phobic. The phobia grows with each time they subject themselves to treatment.

Even if the dentist uses large amounts of anaesthetic the patient will probably still experience pain, if the patient is using 'projection' as a defence against his or her guilt of being afraid. It is not possible to anaesthetize a drill, sound of a drill or even a needle. I have often shown an experiment where I place a coin on the back of a patient's hand, *[The patient should have a high hypnotic capacity and be capable of producing both dissociation and anaesthesia.]* and in a state of hypnosis I tell them that all the sensitivity of their hand is moving into the coin, leaving their hand under the coin quite numb. I draw round the coin and then remove it repeating as I take away the coin I am also taking away their sensitivity of their hand with the coin. I place the coin some distance away. In a high capacity patient it is then very possible to stick a needle into the hand, where the coin was, without the patient feeling anything. If ,however, you prick the coin which you have placed some distance away, provided the patient knows that you have pricked the coin, they will feel pain. I have done this demonstration with a boy, who when I pricked the coin with a needle, let out a yell, and when asked did that hurt he replied 'Yes and it's bleeding.' Sure enough his hand was bleeding where the coin had been. A friend who was watching this experiment, when he saw the blood on the back of the boy's hand, said 'I'm getting out of here. 'I just said 'I'll come with you!' I also did the same experiment with a lighted cigarette and when I touched the coin [which was quite a distance away from the hand] with the cigarette, the patient's hand burned. I have only been able to do this with two very high hypnotic capacity patients. The patient's burn took a week to heal.

Patients using 'projection' as a defence are doing to the drill, sound of the drill or the needle, exactly what I was doing to the coin in the above experiment. Just as you can't anaesthetize a coin, neither can you anaesthetize a drill, sound of a drill or a needle, so if the patient is using 'projection' they will experience pain if any of these instruments are used.

I hope this shows how complicated it can be to treat dental phobics.

One of the ways in which dental phobias develop is to have a bad experience at a previous dental visit, although I have found this to be much less common than one might expect, especially in cases where there has been no previous repression of 'primal pain.' *[In patients who can cuddle both parents it seems much more possible to have a bad experience and get over it without developing a phobia.]*

If the phobia is not too inhibiting one of the best ways to help a patient to have their dental treatment is to give them a distraction technique. I explain the technique to the patient by telling them the following little story. 'I have a nice car but I don't really know how it works, so if it needs a service, or it is not going very well, I take it to a garage who I have found I can trust and ask then to put it right. If I were to stay there while they were fixing my car, and if the mechanic were to take a large spanner and a hammer and he was to hit the spanner very hard with the hammer to loosen a nut, I might just be a little concerned for my car. To avoid this I take my car to the garage and leave it there while I get on with my own work at my consulting rooms. Because I don't see what is happening to my car I'm not too concerned for its safety, and in any case I trust the garage to know what to do for the best for my car.

You can't do your own teeth so why don't you find a way to trust me to do them for you. Then when you trust me, take your mind away somewhere, where it can enjoy itself, while you leave your teeth here with me for a service. While you don't see what I'm doing to help your teeth you needn't be afraid. If you pay very good attention to everything that I'm doing to your teeth then naturally you are going to notice everything that I'm doing much more. You are afraid of what I'm doing, so why make yourself more afraid by paying too much attention to what I have to do to service your teeth. Take your mind away and enjoy yourself, and leave me to worry about your teeth.'

I find most dental phobics who have a medium or high hypnotic capacity can do this quite easily. They can watch their favourite T.V. programme, have their dream holiday, play their best sport, look at their most lovely garden, paintings, or any pastime that completely absorbs their thinking, while their teeth are being attended to. This way they don't even notice their treatment. When the patient is absorbed in their own fantasy, I always tell them that as long as they are in that fantasy they won't be bothered at all by what I'm doing. You need no more suggestions than that. Don't even mention rude four letter words like pain, fear, hurt, otherwise the patient will have to access the meaning of those words to know what they mean, and having accessed them probably feel them.

I well remember doing two fillings for a young man who was very frightened. He was a high capacity hypnotic patient who I had dreaming about some sport he liked doing while I drilled his first tooth. I didn't use any anaesthetic and after finishing the drilling of the first tooth I asked him to rinse his mouth out. After he had done that he said 'That was great, I didn't feel anything, but I'm not convinced that the cavity was very deep so perhaps I wouldn't have felt anything anyway.' Like a fool falling into a trap I assured him that the cavity was fairly deep and he had been very good in distracting himself from feeling any pain. When I came to drill the second tooth there was no way I could get him to distract himself sufficiently to not feel pain, and I had to use an anaesthetic. First of all I had said the cavity was deep, I had also mentioned the word pain, so to access what that meant he had to think about that so in spite of being very successful with the first tooth there was no way he was able to distract from what that meant for the second tooth because of his fear. I had just screwed up the hypnotic distraction by what I had said. This taught me the great importance of thinking what you say to anyone in a hypnotic state.

The first dental case I ever treated with hypnosis was a little girl of about nine years of age, called Elizabeth, who came to me and said she was very frightened to have any dental treatment because she had had a bad experience at another dentist who had been very aggressive towards her. He had not hurt her but he shouted at her for being afraid. I did an examination and found she had four fillings to do. I asked her if she would like to have them numbed to have them done, and she replied 'Yes'. I gave her an injection of local anaesthetic for one side which had two fillings to be done. While I was waiting for the anaesthetic to work she turned very pale and then fainted. I put the chair back so that her head was down and she came round. She was promptly sick over everything and cried. I got no treatment done at all on that first visit. I had just been on my first weekend course to learn about hypnosis so I asked her mother if I could try some hypnosis on another occasion. Both her mother and Elizabeth thought that might be a good idea, so my receptionist fixed her up with another appointment while I cleaned up the sick.

The next time she came into my consulting rooms Elizabeth looked very apprehensive but said she was willing to give hypnosis a go. I did a 'balloon induction' technique and she fortunately went into a very good trance state. I didn't know anything about capacity, at that time, but in retrospect she must have been a high capacity subject. When her hand was up high in the air with her eyes closed I suggested that when I snapped my fingers her hand would drop and she would feel she was at her own home, in her favourite chair in front of the television set. I snapped my fingers and her hand dropped and she indicated by nodding her head that she could see her T.V. set. I asked her to turn it on and when she could see her favourite programme she was to nod her head again. Fairly quickly she nodded her head, so I then just said that so long as she was watching the programme she would hardly notice what I was doing and nothing would bother her. I asked her to open her mouth and proceeded to drill and fill her four teeth. Throughout she remained a good pink colour and had a smile on her face. I didn't use any anaesthetic and she said afterwards she was very surprised that I had done all her fillings as she had felt nothing and thought I had only done one. I felt very good about it too.

I had another child who was watching an imagined television programme called 'Daktari' while I was drilling a particularly deep cavity in a lower molar tooth. All of a sudden she opened her eyes and I thought that the sensation of pain had broken her trance, so I immediately stopped drilling and asked her how she was. She replied that she was fine. I asked her what she was doing and she replied, most indignantly, that she was watching 'Daktari' on television. She continued to watch her imagined programme of 'Daktari' with her eyes open and still in trance while I proceeded to finish her filling.

Fairly quickly I found I could treat most of the dental phobics in this way. A word of warning though, you can easily hypnotise most children but if they don't want the treatment you can't keep them hypnotized to do the treatment. Some children don't want fillings and it isn't possible to keep them in trance to do fillings if they don't want them. It isn't possible to make anyone stay in trance if they don't want whatever you are trying to hypnotise them for.

There, however, remain a few dental phobics, in my experience, who want dental treatment but the above technique won't work. It won't work when the patient has too large a repressed primal pain making them phobic of any possible painful experience. I will describe a few of them, with the way I solved their phobias.

Joan was referred to me by another of my patients, as a person who was just too scared to have any dental treatment. She had neglected her teeth for some years because of her terror, but now she was having a little pain from her teeth. When I saw her she said that she had always been scared of the dentist and in the past she had always been dragged along by her mother, but her mother had died some years back. Since then, as her fear had seemed to get steadily worse, she had been avoiding any contact with the dentist. She was thirty-five years old, single and living with her elderly father. Joan was a quiet, nervous, but very intelligent person. She said she was so scared she didn't think she could let me even look at her teeth let alone touch or drill them.

I tried a distraction technique but got nowhere, she was just too scared to stay in hypnosis. I had her dream in hypnosis that she was a film star and we were making a film about a dentist and she was the patient, and as we were just making a film she wouldn't be scared. She could just go through the dream and I managed to do a dental inspection of her mouth and found she had five teeth that needed filling, as well as an abscess on a front tooth which was the one giving pain. She was too scared, however to stay in the dream for me to do anything else in the way of dental treatment. I prescribed some penicillin for the abscess.

She had a high hypnotic capacity and could produce analgesia in her hand. I showed her how good she was at controlling pain by placing a needle through her hand when she had made it numb and had her look at her hand with the needle sticking through. She was amazed because she hadn't felt the needle at all and said she wouldn't have believed it if she hadn't seen it for herself. This, however, made no difference to her dental phobia, she was still just as scared.

In trance I had her review her previous dental experiences, but, although her fear had been great in all of them, she couldn't recall any of them as being really physically traumatic. Neither could she remember any of them as being psychologically traumatic, apart from the fear. I then set up an ideo-motor finger response and asked her unconscious mind to lift her finger, while we did an age regression, if at any age she experienced the same uncontrollable fear that she associated with dental treatment.

While she was imagining she was eleven years old, in the regression, her ideo-motor finger rose in the air. When I asked her what was happening to her she said she had just moved up into the senior school and it was her first day there. She was terrified and worried, but a friend had moved up with her so it wasn't too bad. If her friend hadn't been there with her she thought she wouldn't have been able to cope. I took her back even further and when we came to seven years of age her finger rose once again. This time she had just started at the boarding school in the junior section. Once again a friend had also started with her, but without her friend she said she would have died. *[I believe that separation from her parents by having to go to boarding school at such an early age had resulted in her being a very nervous person. I find this is a common result, especially in anyone with a first line trauma (Birth trauma) It is just another reinforcement of the original separation trauma.]* At five years of age when she first started day school her ideo-motor finger again rose showing that she had experienced high anxiety at that separation from mother.

I decided to take her back to birth, with the safeguard that she would only experience the level of anxiety which she could take with my help as I would be with her all the time. She found the birth experience terrifying. She was trapped and couldn't move, everything was out of control, she was being 'killed off'. Everything she did seemed to make it worse. She was trembling, shaking, quivering, crying and sobbing. I just comforted her and said it will be alright and you'll get out and it will soon be over. She began to shiver and said it was cold *[A sign she had got 'out'. 'Out' is often colder than in the womb]* She said she couldn't breath it was very dark and hard and she was dying and it was all too much and terrifying.

After a while she said it is better, it's soft and warm and I feel better. I don't feel quite so scared. I comforted her and gradually brought her back to the present day reasssuring her it is over and she never need feel so scared again. Before I terminated the trance, I gave her the option to forget anything that had been too traumatic for her to remember. On waking she remembered it all. She still felt shaky so I gave her a cup of coffee and asked her if she knew what had really happened at her birth. She didn't know.

On returning for her next visit she was very excited and said that she had asked her father if he knew what had happened at her birth. He had told her her mother had had a very difficult delivery. *[If it's difficult for mother it's even more difficult for the baby, but parents don't like to admit that because it generally makes them feel guilty. It's not their fault but unconsciously that makes them feel guilty. Sometimes they will even say it was terrible for me but you were alright. How could that happen?]* Joan had been delivered by a midwife, the doctor wasn't present. The midwife had difficulty in establishing a good breathing rhythm and they thought Joan might die. The midwife suggested Joan should be placed somewhere warm. They put her in the airing cupboard on the boards next to the boiler. They didn't have an open fire, and that was the only place they could think of that was very warm. After a short while she had recovered and they took her out of the airing cupboard and put her in her cot. Mother was too weak after the very difficult birth to be of any help at the time.

Joan claimed she now felt somehow different inside, after re-living her birth and the experience being confirmed by being told about it by her father. She said she felt much more calm and peaceful altogether. I took her in hypnotic dream through the other separation times in her life and showed her how this first separation had compounded her fear at each of those times. She then remembered a visit to the dentist she had experienced when she was only about four years old. She had gone to have a tooth out by gas. She was very frightened and the nurse took her away quite forcibly from her mother and dragged her into the surgery. She had been plonked into a hard chair and a mask had been placed onto her face. She felt she couldn't breath and was going to die. When she woke up she had blood in her mouth and she was terrified. Her phobia had started after that. This dental experience only re-enforced her first birth trauma. First of all came the aggressive separation from mother in the waiting room. Then she was put in a hard chair and when the mask was put on her face she couldn't breath *[The same at birth, she had difficulty in establishing a good breathing rhythm.]* She thought she was dying. *[The same at birth.]* She had blood in her mouth when she came too after the extraction. *[She probably had mucous and blood in her mouth at birth.]* All the circumstances were too alike to not form strong concepts. When we discussed this in the waking state she said she now realized that her fear at the dentist's was of being trapped and not being able to control anything and a fear of dying. This was her birth fear. *[I have found this fear to be the most common concept in dental phobics, and probably learned at birth.]*

We discussed her dental treatment with this new information and I explained that when I was doing her treatment if she wanted to stop it she could do so, so she would have some control. She said she would like to try to have her fillings done. I induced a trance state and had her hallucinate that she was at her favourite holiday place on the Orkney Isles with her little dog, whom she loved, as company, and also any other friends she would like to have with her. *[In her regression to her first day at school a friend had been with her and made it better for her.]* I told her that as long as she was there nothing I was doing would bother her. The spray from the water pistol that I would clean the bad from her tooth would just be like a warm sea fret, and the noise like the wind blowing off the sea. I then proceeded to do her five fillings without any bother and opened up her abscessed tooth to drain the abscess. When it was over she was quite amazed that I had done the five fillings as she had felt nothing and had been relaxed and calm all the time. I made another appointment and finished a root filling on her front abscessed tooth which again was uneventful.

Mrs. Anne Price was referred to me as an 'impossible dental phobic. She is an attractive thirty-five year old housewife and mother. When I saw her for the very first time she seemed extremely tense, in spite of the fact that I was seeing her in my psychotherapy room and not in my dental consulting room. She is happily married with two children, but she had suffered post-natal depression with both children. She had contemplated suicide as a 'way out' during these two bouts of depression, but she said she had not attempted anything. During that time of depression she was 'no use to anyone' and was ashamed of her feelings towards her children whom she loved, but she just couldn't show it to them, or express any of her feelings. She often felt very alone, even now, in spite of the fact that she had a loving husband and two lovely children.

She had been afraid of the dentist all her life but had no conscious memory of any exceptionally traumatic experiences, as she put it. All her visits were traumatic, because of her fear, even though no one had ever hurt her. She had not been able to have any dental treatment for about fifteen years, which coincided with the birth of her first child. She was ashamed of her mouth and said she dare not smile in public. She was slightly agoraphobic and quite claustrophobic. If she went to the theatre she had to sit next to the exit sign on the end of a row. She was afraid of travelling on buses and quite often felt that she 'Had to get out' of a place. This 'Had to get out' feeling is typical of first-line traumas. [See my first book 'How to become the Parent you never Had'.]

Anne was a medium to high capacity hypnotic subject. The ideo-motor finger technique showed no specific trauma connected with her dental phobia except at the birth of her two children and her own birth. *[The same anxiety was experienced at these times as she experienced at the dentists.]* Her fear was of being hurt, with absolutely no way of controlling it.

With hypnotic behaviour therapy to boost Anne's ego and using a distraction technique of imagining herself in a favourite place she thought she would like to 'try' to get into the dental chair. *['Try' was Anne's word. 'Try' is a very negative word, it insinuates it may be difficult, and you may not succeed.]* She was much more relaxed when she entered the dental consulting room and she sat in the chair with no difficulty. I asked her to concentrate on her favourite place as she had done in the psychotherapy room. When, however, I tried to look into her mouth she panicked and broke trance insisting she 'had to get out' of the dental room.

We abandoned all attempts at dentistry and returned to the psychotherapy room to work on her 'Had to get out' feeling. I had her review the Marathon she had won to be here with all the positive anchor feelings connected with that. [See my first book.] I had her do the exercises for that, as in my first book, for no more that two minutes every two hours of her waking day. She did those exercises for two weeks until she began to feel all of the intended feelings.

I then had her dream she was in a cinema watching a film of her birth while she was dissociated form her body. [See my first book.] She was to take her adult mind and persuade her birthing self that her baby self was safe and would get out alive and whole and unharmed. That everyone concerned with the birth wanted her to be well, alive, healthy and unharmed. And that her baby self did in fact get out well, safe, and unharmed and that the birth is now over and she never need feel so afraid again about being trapped.

Anne was taught to review her birth, using auto-hypnosis every day, with all the reassurances of the fact that she endured it without harm, and it's now over and she need never again feel so strongly that she has to get out of anywhere. We repeated this exercise on five occasions after which, without any suggestions about her dental treatment, Anne offered to undergo her dental treatment. This was completed uneventfully and the patient experienced many other spin off beneficial side effects from her treatment.

The third and last case of dental phobia I would like to describe is probably the worst dental phobic I have ever encountered. Rebecca was referred to me from a special clinic at the dental hospital for hair-lips and cleft-palate patients. She had had a repair done to her lip and palate many years previously, and the plastic surgeons wished to continue with a further cosmetic repair on her lip and nose. The particular surgeon said he would not do this until she was made dentally fit. She was terrified of having the operation in the first place and would not consent to having any dental treatment because she was terrified of that too.

She spoke to a consultant at the clinic who promised her he would give her an intravenous injection to put her to sleep so that she would be unconscious and totally unaware while he did all her necessary dental treatment. However she completely refused to have anything to do with it as she said she could not possibly face up to any dental treatment. After a number of unsuccessful attempts to persuade her, about six in all, he decided to refer her to me.

Rebecca was eighteen years old, a very pleasant girl, who said she wanted to join the woman's police force. They, however, said they would not accept her until after she had had her plastic surgery. She insisted she wanted to join the force but didn't know how she was going to face up to having her dentistry, or the operation to her lip and nose. I saw her for a total of eight visits before doing her dental treatment. She was a high capacity hypnotic subject and I decided that I would have to use regression to her previous traumas to rebuild her concepts about surgery in order to help her. Her existing concepts were too strong to use distraction to any effect.

During her regression she experienced herself in the womb when her fingers went immediately up to, and in her mouth. The plastic surgeon thought that may have been the reason why she had a hair-lip and cleft-palate in the first place. While she was reliving the womb experience it was almost impossible to remove her fingers from her mouth. Her birth experience was very traumatic with a very strong 'wipe out' feeling. I had to rebuild those concepts for her. On another visit she re-experienced her first lip and palate repair operation. When this was done she had had to have her hands tied at her sides so that she couldn't put them in her mouth. As a few days old baby she found this a very frightening experience and she cried a lot while reliving it. There were quite a lot of concepts about that that we had to change.

On reliving these experiences and releasing the negative emotions attached to them, and building new concepts about them, she felt a little more confident in herself. On another session she relived all the times at school when she had refused to have the injections for small-pox, scarlet fever etc. by hiding in the toilet and refusing to come out. In those days we all used to have those injections as a matter of rule. She also relived all the times the other children had teased her about her appearance, and how that had hurt her. We had to give her some new concepts about that too.

On one visit I asked her who had hurt her the most. She replied her mother for having her. She sobbed she wished she had never been born. [*The 'Blame Game'* **see my first book.**] I had to teach her she won a marathon race to be here, so she asked to be here, so she better find a way of making the most of it and stop blaming others for making her life a misery.

We talked in the waking state about how in refusing to have her treatment she didn't have to grow up. *[Not wanting to be here.]* She couldn't get a job until her treatment was done so that was a way of getting back at her mother for having her in the first place. If she continued to play the blame game her personality would never mature. *[The very purpose of life itself]* Her phobia was a useful mask for her feelings of insecurity, inferiority and inadequacy. Her unconscious mind could say I would be O.K. if I could have my operation, but I am too afraid to have that, and I can't help being afraid, so it's not my fault. *[Blame game.]* I explained that it was inevitable that every day would be followed by another and if she put off getting one day wiser every day, by playing the blame game, she would be the one who is hurting herself the most. I also explained that as she had been punishing her mother for eighteen years for something that was not her mother's fault, she should begin to find a better way to live her life.

After eight visits of discussion and regression as above, she asked if I would give her an intravenous anaesthetic and do all her necessary dental treatment. She was reasonably calm and composed when my aneasthetist gave her the injection to put her to sleep, and while asleep I completed all her necessary dental treatment except a scaling and polish. She returned a week later and had her scaling from my hygienist.

She has returned every six months and had all her dental treatment as it became necessary. She also had her plastic surgery to her nose and lip. She also has a job, but not in the police force, and is getting on with her life.

I hope this chapter shows you how and why some people defend their mouths to their detriment and what can be done to help them.

CHAPTER 10

Dentures. Why do some people reject them even when they have no teeth?

There are a few people who have their teeth extracted and when we come to fit them with dentures they find they cannot tolerate them no matter how hard they try. These people represent a very small number of difficult dental patients, but nevertheless they can present quite a problem. I will describe two such patients to illustrate the dynamics behind their behaviour and to show how I helped them to overcome the defences which were preventing them from wearing their dentures.

Emma was referred to me from the dental hospital. She was an attractive twenty-one year old who had had all her teeth extracted by a general dental practitioner about two years before being referred to me. She had neglected her mouth to such an extent that the dentist could do nothing for her except extract all her teeth which were abscessed and so badly decayed that most of them were just roots. He had to use a general anaesthetic to take them out because of her tremendous phobia of any dental treatment.

When her gums had healed and she returned for false teeth, the dentist who had extracted the teeth found he couldn't get anywhere near Emma to take her impressions. After a few aborted attempts he referred her to the dental hospital. At the hospital they found the same difficulty, so they gave her a general anaesthetic, to knock her out, so that they could take her impressions. The hospital then made her some wax bite blocks to register the relationship of one jaw to the other. When they came to try to place these wax bite blocks in Emma's mouth she flatly refused to try them, insisting she couldn't bear to have them anywhere near her mouth. They once again gave her a general anaesthetic and registered her bite. They then made a wax set of teeth for her to try in her mouth but, as you may have expected, she refused to let them insert the wax dentures.

At this late stage the dentists at the hospital decided that if she couldn't put the wax dentures in her mouth she wouldn't be able to wear her finished dentures, so there was little or no point in giving her a general anaesthetic to try these teeth in, to test them for appearance. After many unsuccessful attempts to persuade her to put them in her mouth, they decided that she must be a little unbalanced and ought to see a psychiatrist. Somebody at the hospital suggested she should come to me to see what I may be able to do with hypnosis. She was given the wax dentures, that they had made for her, to bring with her. I tried many of the behaviour techniques which work with most gagging patients.

The first technique I tried was to use a 'sick stick'. A 'sick stick' can be made from a broom handle or a piece of copper piping, about an inch thick and eighteen inches long, which has been polished to look attractive, with a mark somewhere on the middle. You tell the patient to grip this stick at both ends with their hands held out at arms length in front of them. They are then to stare as hard as they can at the mark in the middle of the 'sick stick'. While they are doing that, you tell them, very convincingly, that it is impossible to retch while they continue to grip the stick and look at the mark. This is using a distraction technique with the suggestion that they can't retch, which will make it possible to take impressions in most retching dental patients without any difficulty. What better way, than to give a patient an eighteen inch rigid phallic symbol to grip hard to distract them. Emma would open her mouth while she gripped the stick but when I approached her with the wax dentures to try them in, she immediately dropped the stick and closed her mouth. She insisted it would not be possible for her to have the dentures put into her mouth without her choking.

I then did a capacity test and found to my delight and

surprise that Emma was a high capacity hypnotic subject. In a deep trance I had her hallucinate that she was lying on a sandy beach feeling the warm sun making her sleepy and very relaxed and calm and confident. While she was feeling so relaxed and confident I told her that as long as she was there on that beach she would not be bothered by anything that I was doing near her mouth. I asked her to gently open her mouth. She opened it wide but as I approached her mouth with the dentures she broke trance, insisting it was still impossible for her to have the dentures in her mouth without choking. This once again shows clearly that it isn't possible to make anyone do anything in hypnosis that they do not want to do. It also gave me a clue that she had a strong unconscious reason for not putting her dentures into her mouth.

The next time she came I asked her to bring a blank cassette tape, so that I could give her a tape recording of the treatment I was proposing to do with her. When she came into my consulting room I asked her who her favourite film actress was. Much to my surprise she said 'Elizabeth Taylor.' I was surprised because Elizabeth Taylor was my favourite actress as she was of my era. I asked her if Elizabeth Taylor was really her favourite actress and she said she didn't know why she had picked her because she didn't really know Elizabeth Taylor that well. I knew why she had picked Elizabeth Taylor but I didn't know how I had projected that actress on to Emma. I didn't even know I was thinking of Elizabeth Taylor at the time I asked her the question. Anyhow, as she had picked Elizabeth Taylor as her actress I told her to think of Richard Burton as an actor.

I then induced a deep trance in Emma and encouraged her to hallucinate that she was a stand-in for Elizabeth Taylor and I was a stand-in for Richard Burton. We were all in a film studio making a movie. In this scene Richard Burton was a dentist and Elizabeth was going to have her teeth fixed by him. I set up an ideo-motor finger response in Emma's index finger so that any time Emma was feeling nervous her finger would rise. Emma and I then were to watch Richard fixing some dentures for Elizabeth. As it was just a film Emma would be able to watch Elizabeth having some dentures fixed by Richard without feeling nervous at all. This was confirmed by Emma's ideo-motor finger keeping very still and not rising at all throughout the scene. I taped the whole scene including the hypnotic induction of Emma, and the fact that she had been able to watch Elizabeth have her teeth fixed by Richard without feeling the least bit nervous, together with the terminating of Emma's trance. I gave Emma the cassette and told her to listen to it at least once every day for the next week.

In a week's time she returned and I again helped her into an altered state [Hypnosis] and went through the scene once more, but this time Elizabeth had a sore throat and couldn't do the scene. As Emma was her stand-in for this scene, she would have to take the part where Richard Burton was fixing her teeth. Almost immediately Emma's ideo-motor finger started to rise even though I hadn't deliberately set it to rise if she was experiencing anxiety. Emma was reassured that it was just a film and we were not actually going to do anything. Since it was only a film and Richard Burton was her co-star it would be great fun and pleasurable to have him fix her teeth, and she need not be afraid. Emma was then taken in hypnotic dream through the scene where Richard was trying in some new teeth for her. She managed to get through this scene without her ideo-motor finger rising.

This was also taped with the induction, the dental scene where Emma had her teeth fixed by Richard B. and the termination of the trance. At the end of this treatment Emma was given the tape and asked to play it to herself every day for the next week.

On returning a week later, she seemed much more cheerful and confident when she entered the consulting room. I again helped her into an altered state and this week Elizabeth Taylor still had a bad throat and Richard Burton also was off sick. As I was his stand in we did the scene with Emma having her teeth fixed by me this time. She again was able to get through this scene without her ideo-motor finger rising with anxiety. This was again taped and given to her to play to herself every day for the next week.

The next time she returned we went into my dental consulting room and she quite happily sat in my dental chair without any sign of fear. I rehypnotised her and said we would just go through the scene where I would try her teeth in for her. After going through the scene I informed her we would have to do a retake and try to make it more real for the film. When she was calm and happy and still in an altered state I asked her to gently open her mouth and I would just try her dentures in. As I approached her with the real wax try in teeth she broke trance and said she couldn't go through with it. This was the final time I needed convincing that you can't make anyone do anything in hypnosis that they are unwilling to do out of hypnosis. I decided that if we were going to succeed with Emma I was going to have to find out why she didn't want to wear false teeth.

The next time she came I helped her into as deep a trance as was possible for her and suggested that when I snapped my fingers she would have a dream that would help us both know some of the reason why she thought she couldn't wear her dentures. When I snapped my fingers I watched her closed eyelids and noticed a 'Rapid Eye Movement' [R.E.M.] indicating she was dreaming. When the eye movement stopped I asked her to describe her dream and she burst into tears. I encouraged her to cry telling her it was safe to do that now and even as she told me her dream she could cry even harder to release her pent up feelings. She sobbed and said 'I'm not a very nice person. I have been unpleasant all of my life. I have deliberately done bad things to get out of doing anything I didn't want to do, no matter who I hurt doing that. I broke off my engagement with my fiance for no real reason. I just felt I didn't want him anymore. He didn't do anything to make me do that, and he and my mother were very upset.

She said she had made herself physically sick many times to get out of having to do things she had not wanted to do. I just let her cry until she stopped on her own accord. When she stopped I brought her out of trance with the safeguard that she would only remember that which she felt strong enough to feel at this moment in time. When she opened her eyes she said she could remember everything, but she said she didn't know what all that had to do with not being able to wear her dentures. She had at least given me a clue that she probably was refusing to wear them for some unconscious reason that had nothing directly to do with wearing dentures. This was the first piece of the puzzle.

The next time she came I did an age regression with hypnosis and set up an ideo-motor finger response for the finger to rise when we reached an age when she had got out of doing something she hadn't wanted to do by being sick. She had avoided going to school on a number of occasions, exams, tests, injections by the doctor, visits to her aunts, helping her mother and a whole range of other things. When we reached the age of four she burst into tears and she was encouraged to cry while she told me what was upsetting her at four years of age. She said 'My father is ill and I am being sent to my granny's and I'm worried about my daddy. I don't know what is happening and my granny says I have to stay here for the time being. I seem to have been at my granny's for a few weeks but I'm going home now'. With even more sobs she cried 'My daddy isn't at home and every time I ask my mummy where he is she just cries and says he has gone away. I know what happened now he died. This is the first time I have ever cried about that' and she burst into uncontrollable tears. After a while she stopped and said she felt a little better. By this time she had broken trance herself and come back to the present day, but just in case I asked her how old she was and she said 'twenty-one', so we just talked about it. She said 'Obviously my father died while I was at my granny's and my mother was so upset she couldn't tell me about it. When I eventually did find out, he had been gone for such a long time I couldn't feel anything so today is the first time I have been able to cry about it. You know somehow I feel a lot better about it now.' Another clue in the puzzle.

She said she felt that she had been choking back her tears all this time and now that she had been able to cry about it she felt as though a burden had been lifted from her mind. I suggested that she might like to try her dentures in, now that

she had got that off her mind, so she let me put the bottom
ones in her mouth but when I came to try the top ones she
said she couldn't do that.

At this time I was due to go to Chicago to attend a
conference of the American Society of Clinical Hypnosis.
While I was there I had the good fortune to meet Calvert
Stein and his delightful wife Lucille. Sometimes when you
are dealing with a difficult case you are too near the wood to
see the trees and it's good to get away and share your
problem with like minds. The Steins and I were walking
along the shores of lake Michigan and I was telling them
about Emma when Lucille said 'Why don't you ask her who
she would bite if she had some teeth in.'

I did just that when I returned. I helped Emma into a trance
state and said *'I want you to imagine you have some teeth in your
mouth and you want to bite someone. Who do you think you would
like to bite?'*
Emma replied immediately without thinking 'my mother.'
The key piece of the puzzle was now revealed. Emma's
mother was being punished for not letting Emma feel the
grief over her father's death. An ideo-motor finger response
was set up with a finger to rise for 'Yes' and another to rise
for 'No'. The following questions were then asked. *'Do you
think you are an unpleasant person because you have been
punishing your mother for not letting you cry over your father's
death all this time?'*
Her 'Yes' finger rose.
*'Did you do badly at school because your mother wanted you to do
well?'*
Her 'Yes' finger rose.
*'Was your mother delighted with your fiance when you got
engaged?'*
Her 'Yes' finger rose'.
*'Did you break off your engagement because your mother was so
pleased at your engagement and you wanted to hurt her so you broke
it off?'*
Her 'Yes' finger rose.
'Is your mother worried about you not wearing any false teeth?'
Her 'Yes' finger rose.

'Are you not wearing teeth to punish your mother?'
Her 'Yes' finger rose.
'Just suppose you had done something wrong, Do you think five years would be a long enough sentence to serve?'
Her 'Yes' finger rose.
'If you did something very bad do you think ten years would be a long enough sentence?'
Her 'Yes finger rose.
'Do you realise that you have been punishing your mother for not letting you grieve over your father's death for seventeen years now?'
Her 'Yes' finger rose slowly after a little pause.
'Don't you think it's about time you forgave her?'
Her 'Yes' finger rose quite quickly this time.
'Wouldn't you be more comfortable yourself if you forgave her? You could then like yourself much more if you forgave her.'
Her 'Yes ' finger rose quickly.
'If you have forgiven her you have no reason to not wear your teeth have you?'
Her 'Yes' finger rose slowly.
'Would you like to try them in then?'
She said 'yes' verbally, and added she had not consciously been aware that she couldn't wear her teeth because she was punishing her mother, or any of the other questions I had asked her. In fact she was very surprised at some of the answers her finger had given. I explained that if she had been aware of the facts I was sure she would have forgiven her mother long ago, and not done many of the things that her unconscious mind had made her do. This was just another example of the way the unconscious mind's efforts to help had become the problem. [See my first book **'How to Become The Parent You Never Had.'**]

I put both sets of teeth [Upper and lower] into her mouth and made the necessary corrections so that I could get my mechanic to process them into plastic. This was done and the next week I fitted her finished dentures which looked very good. She took them away with her and reported that at first she had only been able to wear the upper one, but now she is able to wear both satisfactorily.

The other case I would like to describe was a delightful lady called Grace Richards. She was sent to me by another consultant in the denture department of the Dental Hospital. A copy of his letter follows.

Dear Mr. Graham,
　　　　　re: Grace Richards
　　　　　Hartford House,
　　　　　Newburn on Tyne. D.O.B. 17.6.28

I have being seeing Miss Richards who was referred to me by Mr. Brown. I have spoken to Mr. Brown on the telephone today and discussed Miss Richards, and the possibility of referring her to yourself. He has no objections, and in fact seemed to think it would be a good idea. He said he had heard of you and had considered sending her to you himself. As you will be aware Miss Richards is very unhappy wearing a partial upper denture and suffers nausea and retching. The partial denture itself is very satisfactory from a technical point of view, and I am concerned both about her not being able to wear it and the probability of her having to have more extensive dentures in the years to come.

I gather you are happy to examine her to see if hypnosis would help, and I am only too pleased to give my blessing to the project as I really think if we do not improve this intolerance in the near future we will have considerable problems.

　　　　　　　　　　Yours sincerely,

　　　　　　　　　　Consultant Prosthetic Dept.
　　　　　　　　　　Dental Hospital.

Miss Richards was a delightful lady who was extremely well groomed and very young looking for her age. She was fifty-three years old. She had been a little depressed in the past and had seen a consultant psychiatrist friend of mine who had helped her a lot with her depression. She had had to have some upper teeth extracted recently and had a partial chrome cobalt skeleton denture made for the missing teeth, which she was unable to wear for more than a few hours at a time. Even then when she was wearing it she felt sick and wanted to retch all the time, and as soon as she was alone she would take it out to get some comfort. She had tried to get used to the denture for a year now and the consultant at the hospital had told her that there was nothing wrong with the denture and she would just have to persevere. She insisted she had tried but she couldn't tolerate it for more than a few hours. She said when I have it in my mouth I'm always waiting for the time when I can take it out. *[Programming herself to be unable to wear it.]*

As she insisted she wanted to be able to wear these dentures, I decided we would have to find out why her unconscious mind was rejecting them, and making her unable to tolerate them. I tested her for hypnotic capacity and found her to be medium to high with very little resistance, which meant that I should be able to do some analysis with Miss Richards.

I made her another appointment and on her return I helped her into an altered state of consciousness and decided that I should see if there was any birth trauma because of her reported depression. I regressed her back to the 17th. of June 1928 which was the date of birth on the dental consultants letter to me, and also the date she had given to my receptionist who had made her record card out. I started a dream induction for birth and she became irritated and said 'no that's not my birth it was the 17th of June 1918.' A bell rang in my head, the puzzle was solved by a mistake, or at least I had not intended to solve it that way. She had deliberately falsified her date of birth on at least two occasions, once to the hospital and once to my receptionist. Obviously she was afraid of getting old and her real age was sixty-three not fifty-three. She had very skillfully made herself up to not even look fifty-three let alone sixty-three. I abandoned the attempted birth dream and instead set up an ideo-motor finger response for her finger to rise for a 'Yes' answer and also another finger for 'No'.

'I asked her unconscious if her parents had had dentures when they were old?'

Her 'Yes' finger rose.
'I asked her if she was afraid of dying?' [Both her parents had died and she had looked after them to the end.]
Her 'Yes' finger rose.
'I asked her if she associated dentures with getting old?'
Her 'Yes' finger rose.
'I asked her if she associated dentures with dying?'
Her 'Yes' finger rose.

People with false teeth, when they are ill or close to death, often take their teeth out and look suddenly very much older because their faces fall in and they look gaunt and very ill. Their relatives, seeing them with their teeth out on a cupboard at the bedside, often associate the absence of teeth, and indirectly the teeth themselves, with old age and dying. This sticks in the relative's unconscious mind. At least it had in Miss Richard's mind. No wonder she couldn't wear her teeth, she didn't want to look old and was afraid of dying and unconsciously associated false teeth with both. These thoughts made her sick and she just wanted to take her teeth out so that they didn't remind her of death and growing old. I have subsequently found this dynamic factor in other cases of older people who won't wear their dentures.

I had to reframe Miss Richard's associations with false teeth. I asked her unconscious mind to think of false teeth like any other aid to good grooming, like having her hair done, [It was well cut and styled] or like foundation cream, blusher and lipstick. [She was very skillfully made up.] Dentures were just another form of cosmetic that would help her to look younger and fitter. After a short while she was able to wear her dentures without any rejection of them and she stopped wanting to take them out of her mouth as soon as she arrived home. In fact, a very short period after this treatment, she reported that she didn't even notice she was wearing them. I also gave her some help for her depression and her fear of growing old and dying but that is outside the reference of this chapter.

I hope these two cases have shown you how complex an organ the mouth may be, and the last two chapters show how we sometimes defend our mouths to our detriment.

CHAPTER 11

Conclusions.

In part 1. of this book I have tried to show how we learn something and then relegate it to our unconscious mind. This is not such a ridiculous notion if you think about it. If we had to go around thinking about everything we had learned in our conscious mind, fairly soon it would become cluttered up. For example, if I were to ask any normal adult who was sitting down to stand up and walk across the room I'm sure they would be able to do that. If, when they had walked across the room, I was to ask them how they did that I am sure very few, if any, would be able to tell me. If they could talk intelligently at the age of nine months, when they were learning to take one step after another, and I were to ask them how they walked across the room then I'm sure they would be able to tell me how they did it, otherwise they would fall down. Once they have walked a number of times they relegate the 'how' to their unconscious mind so that their conscious mind is left clear to think of more important and current things. Once they have learned to walk easily they hardly ever go back to crawling, it's too easy to walk. This method of learning is an example of operant conditioning, it has a reward at the end. The reward is, it is much easier to get from one place to another by walking rather that crawling.

Another example which clearly shows the necessity to consciously think first and then relegate to the unconscious the behaviour, is when learning to drive a car. When you first start learning to drive a car you have to think what you are doing with your hands, as in steering or changing gear. At the same time you have to know what your feet are doing

135

with the clutch or brake or accelerator, while at the same time you have to keep a look out with your eyes on the road ahead and in the mirror for the road behind. When you first begin to do this you think you will never be able to do all those things together and drive safely. In fact you drive more safely when you do relegate those actions to your unconscious, and you don't have to think consciously what you are doing.

Most of the things I have talked about in the first part of this book are learned behaviours which served a very useful purpose at the time they were learned, and when learned, they were relegated to the unconscious memory. Unfortunately many of them still influenced the behaviour long after the circumstances had changed and the unconscious behaviour itself then became the problem. Many things in our memory are readily available to our conscious, but some are not easily made conscious. Whether the memory is accessible or not, it can act as a dynamic force, influencing and moulding our behaviour without our even being aware of the memory. This is why the ideo-motor finger response works. To think about anything we have to access our memory to identify the thing we are trying to think about. We do this both consciously and at the same time unconsciously. This can be seen when you ask a person a question with an answer of yes or no. If the answer is yes the person says yes verbally but at the same time they nod their head. If the answer is no they say no and at the same time shake their head. The ideo-motor finger is just another way of nodding or shaking the head. You don't have to know the answer consciously to get an ideo-motor answer. In fact often the person being asked the question doesn't know the answer consciously.

If however there is a dynamic force affecting behaviour, and there is no behaviour without there being a force making it happen, then there must be a memory somewhere of that force and how it was created. This book is about altering those dynamic forces. We do this in the exercises in this book and learn the new behaviour by Pavlovian conditioning. That is why it is necessary to do the exercises for thirty seconds to one minute every two hours for about twenty days. These exercises can be done with, or without, hypnosis but they will probably be formed more quickly with hypnosis.

After the new Pavlovian conditioned behaviour takes affect with a bit of luck the behaviour should become learned by operant conditioning because it should become easier to live with the new way of functioning. If it isn't, then try something else until it does. The one good thing about this therapy is that it creates new options in life and that is what all therapy should be about.

If we think of the mind as a bio-computer we can compare it with an electronic computer and word processor. To alter a file on a electronic computer you write over the existing file then save the new file. This action removes the old file completely unless you have a back-up file. If you have a back-up file, and you delete the back-up file the old one then doesn't exist any more. The bio-computer we call our mind doesn't work quite like that. When with the exercises we create a new dynamic force. [New file.] This makes a completely new file in the bio-computer, [Mind] but the old one remains along side the new one. What ever happened to us to create a dynamic force happened and can't be undone. We can however relegate the old file to the archives and use the new dynamic forces created by the exercises in this book. If the new file makes life easier and more real it is unlikely that we will resort to the old file again. If this does happen then you will just have to reprogramme yourself over again.

Anchors or anchor situations are what trigger off old files being activated and it may be necessary to recognize the anchors and neutralize them. This can be done by going through the anchor situation in hypnotic dream with the new behaviour and allowing the patients to experience for themselves how much better it is to behave with the newly created behaviour. Anchors are triggering mechanisms described in my first book.

The following exercise in metaphor is a useful way of getting across to the patient the above ideas. This exercise is best done with a therapist and gives a very good indirect way of hypnotising a resistant female patient.

EXERCISE 36.
Changing new for old for women patients.

I have emphasized the important parts in the metaphor in bold print.

Having got my patient comfortably seated with her shoes off and both of her feet flat on the ground I ask her to 'just close your eyes.' Then I say the following to her.

'I would like you, for a moment, to think about your eyes. They are your windows on to the world. You can send messages out from them. You can show love, hate, hunger, anger, fear, guilt, and all your emotions just by looking in different ways. At the same time your eyes can take messages in. When a light beam falls on to your eye the lens at the front of your eye concentrates the beam on to small cells, in the shape of rods and cones, at the back of your eye. These cells as a result of the light being concentrated on them produce certain chemicals. Those chemicals excite the nerve at the back of your eye and create an electrical impulse to pass back along the nerve through the hole in the back of your eyeball into the brain. And still you haven't seen anything. The nerve in the brain then crosses over to the other side of the brain and excites more nerves. And still you haven't seen anything. All this would happen if you were asleep and someone gently opened your eyelid and looked into your eye. If you didn't wake up you wouldn't see anything.

The nerves that have now been excited send an impulse to the visual centre in your brain to alert and wake up that part of your brain and at last you see something. At the same time other nerves send impulses to your memory centre to help you to identify whatever you are now seeing. Your memory centre has millions of little circuits with all sorts of memories.

There was an interesting programme on the television sometime ago about a girl who was blind and the eye surgeons decided if they did an operation on her eyes she may be able to see. They did the operation and when the bandages were removed, much to everyone's delight, she could see. They did some very interesting experiments while the girl was sitting at a table. They placed a cup on the table and asked her if she knew what it was. She didn't know what it was until they pushed it towards her and asked her to pick it up. When her hands touched it she laughed and said it's a cup. She had no visual memory of a cup because she had never seen a cup before, but she had a tactile memory of a cup because she had drunk out of a cup many times and touched a cup many times. As soon as she touched it she recognised it as a cup. **She had to learn all over again what everything looked like before she could visually identify what everything was.**

All our memories are stored in little compartments in our brain. Those compartments could be like your bedroom with wardrobes and a chest of drawers and a dressing table and perhaps a bookshelf for your books. You have specific places to keep all your special things. Sometimes if your things have just been washed, or you have just been looking at them, and you haven't yet had time to put them away, you may need your bedroom, because guests are coming to visit you, and you want to put your guest's coats on your bed while they are with you. You may just push your things into the wardrobe to make the room look tidy for the time being, but after they have gone **you will have to go back and tidy up properly, and put all your things in their proper place.**

One day you may be walking down the high street and while you are passing a little dress shop, there in the window on a model is the most beautiful dress, just your colour and style. You can't believe your luck because it has been reduced from a ridiculous price to a real bargain. You can't resist going in and asking the sales girl if you can try it on. She is pleased to help you and shows you to a changing room and brings the dress. You quickly take off the dress you are wearing and put on the new one and you turn to look at it in the mirror. When you see it a thrill goes right through you. **It fits you perfectly. It does something for you, shows off all your best qualities. It's just your colour.** [When this exercise is over it is often useful to ask what colour the dress was. The colour may give a clue to what is in the patients unconscious mind at the time.] **It seems to bring out your best personality and makes you feel very confident.** You decide to have it, so you take it off and put on the dress you came in with. Taking the new dress to the sales girl you say you will take it, so she wraps it up for you and you pay the money and go out of the shop.

Outside, you can't really believe everything you thought inside the shop, so you hurry home and rush up to your bedroom. There, you pull off the wrapping and **examine the dress again**. It still looks just as good and all the stitching is perfect and there are no marks on it. Quickly you once again take off your dress and try on the new one. It looks even better, **fits you even better than you dared think. You feel a million dollars in it. You are very pleased with yourself.**

You decide you don't want to wear it right now, but will keep it for a special occasion, so you take it carefully off and once again put your old one back on. You go with it to your wardrobe to hang it up but when you open your wardrobe door you find all the hangers are in use. You don't have a spare one to hang your beautiful new dress on so you have to look through all your dresses until you find an old one. **One that doesn't fit any more, that is worn, or out of fashion. One that does nothing for you, or that you have ceased to like. One that doesn't suit your new personality.** When you find one that is no use to you anymore you take it out and place your new one on that hanger and put it carefully in your wardrobe and close the door. **You feel good, even just knowing it is there, when you want it.** You take the old one and send it off to Oxfam, or cut it up for dusters, or just put it in the dustbin.

You feel very pleased with yourself. **It's always necessary, once in a while, to look through your old things and have a good clean out. You throw away the old useless things, which you have accumulated over the years, discarding those which do nothing for you anymore.** Your mind is just like that.'

End of exercise 36.

If the patient is a male who is obviously interested in clothes just substitute a suit for a dress. If however he isn't obviously interested in clothes as many males aren't, then substitute an object from his favourite hobby for the dress and his 'den', office, pigeon-holed desk, for the bedroom, whichever fits.

The above exercise in metaphor sums up all I have to say about the processes described in this book. I thank you for reading it and hope it may have given you more options in your life.

The Exercises.

EXERCISE 1.

Find a comfortable chair preferably with a high back which will support your head. Sit comfortably in the chair and rest your head on the back. Place your feet with your soles flat on the ground. At this point I always suggest that female patients remove their shoes. Ladies tend to take off their shoes when returning home after work, a shopping expedition, an evening out etc. and it is therefore a major aid to their relaxation. Place both your arms comfortably and lightly on each armrest of the chair; if there are no armrests on the chair, place one hand upon each knee. Do not fold your arms or clasp your hands, as both these behaviours are defensive. Look straight ahead of you, then, without altering the position of your head, turn your eyes up to look up towards your eyebrows. Turn them up as high as you can without moving your head. Keeping your eyes turned up close your eyes. (SPIEGEL'S EYEROLL INDUCTION)

Now relax your eyes, let them become so relaxed, so heavy they feel they just won't open, and hang on to that feeling. Now let that feeling spread through the whole of your body. Let your body sink comfortably down into the chair. (ELMAN DEEPENING)

While your body is sinking down into the chair turn your mind inward to look at your mind (GEOFF GRAHAM & N.L.P) Let your mind feel as if it can float. (SPIEGEL)

End of exercise One. This exercise also appears in 'How to Become the Parent You Never Had'

The next exercise also appears in the above book and that exercise is to set up an ideo-motor finger response.

EXERCISE 2.   IDEO-MOTOR FINGER RESPONSES.

When you are talking to someone in a perfectly normal state of consciousness, and you are asking them a question to which they answer 'yes', watch their head. Ask them another question to which they will answer 'yes' and watch their head again. Most people answering 'yes' to a question will not only say 'yes', but at the same time they will nod their head. Ask them without telling them, 'what did they do when they answered the question' and most of them won't have a clue what they did, showing that the nod of the head is an unconscious answer. The same is true of a negative answer when they shake the head.

While people are talking, even in a normal state of consciousness, two parts of their mind are listening, paying attention and answering. The conscious mind is answering by verbally saying 'yes' or 'no', but at the same time the unconscious mind is also answering by nodding or shaking the head. This nodding or shaking of the head is called an ideo-motor response. It is a response from the unconscious mind. We often set this up deliberately so that we can explore the unconscious mind. If we are being affected by something which happened to us long ago, we must have a memory of it somewhere within us; if this were not the case, it would not be affecting us now. This memory, however, is often long since forgotten consciously, but it is still in the unconscious somewhere. We can explore the unconscious mind in an altered state by asking the unconscious to answer our questions by lifting a finger of one of our hands, say the index finger of the left hand, or often it is better to let the unconscious mind choose which finger it will use. It can use one finger for 'yes' and another for 'no', in this way we can ask it yes or no questions. You can even have an 'I don't know' finger, and an 'I don't want to answer' finger, but I feel having too many alternatives often confuses the answer. We are much less used to lying with our finger so we may well get a more honest answer this way. It is not, however, infallible and the finger can lie. So we just ask our unconscious mind if it will answer in this way and if it will, will it please lift a 'yes' finger. One finger should rise.

Establish a 'no' finger in the same way and if you get a response both times you should be able to ask it some more questions that may help you to have more options. It it not so easy to do this by yourself but if it is first done with a therapist many patients can do it by themselves. The skill is often in knowing what to ask it, and what to do about it when you get an answer.

Having now set up an ideo-motor finger response you explain to the patient in the hypnotic state the facts about learned concepts and then you ask the patient's unconscious mind if it will answer questions about any learned concepts which are still active regarding over-eating. If it will answer would it please lift the 'Yes' finger. When the finger lifts, indicating its willingness to respond ask 'Is there a concept in your unconscious mind about having to eat to grow and survive?' 'If there is, the 'yes' finger will rise, if no the 'no' finger will rise'. Make a note of the answer. Go through all thirteen books in the mental library shown above on pages 14 & 15. For number thirteen, ask is there any other concept in your unconscious mind that makes you over-eat? Make a note of all the answers. For each positive answer it is necessary to reframe the concept to a more suitable way of helping the patient to deal with his or her problem without over-eating. The way to do that is shown in the exercises below.

EXERCISE 3.
If there is a positive answer to No.1 contact the part of your mind that is helping you to grow, and thank it for helping you to grow when you were small. When that part of your mind is listening, paying attention and wanting to help, and is willing to negotiate, let it lift your 'Yes' finger. When your finger lifts, remind the part that you have finished growing upwards and the only way you can grow now is outwards, and you don't want to do that.

Would the part of your mind that is helping you to grow please now help you to maintain a healthy weight without growing any more. If it will, let it lift your 'Yes' finger. When the finger rises thank it for agreeing to help you in this new way.

EXERCISE 4.
If there is a positive answer to No.2 and your mind is helping you to cope with loneliness by making you eat to feel less alone, thank it for trying to help you. Ask the part of your mind that is making you eat when you feel lonely, when it is listening, paying attention, wanting to help, and is willing to negotiate, to lift your 'Yes' finger. When the finger lifts, respectfully remind the mind that you would be able to make more friends and be much more confident in meeting new people when you are less fat. Ask it to help you to get, and stay, slimmer, so that you will be confident to go out and meet more friends to be less lonely. When that part agrees to help you in this new way let it lift your 'Yes' finger. When the finger lifts, thank it.

EXERCISE 5.
If your mind is helping you to reduce stress by eating as in No.3, or tension as in No.4 contact that part of your mind, and when it is listening, paying attention, wanting to help, and is willing to negotiate, let it lift your 'Yes' finger. Thank it for trying to help you to cope with stress or tension but respectfully remind it that by making you fat it is now increasing your stress/tension and the way it is trying to help you has become a problem. There are many more efficient ways of reducing stress/tension now that you are older. [See my first book How to Become the Parent You Never Had, chapter 6. pages 68-74.]

Ask the part of your mind that is making you eat to reduce stress/tension to help you in four or five of the alternative ways, as outlined in my first book, instead of making you over-eat. When it is willing to do that, have it indicate its willingness by lifting your 'Yes' finger. When the finger lifts, thank it.

EXERCISE 6.
If you are experiencing an empty feeling in life and your mind is trying to help you cope with that feeling by making

you over-eat in an attempt to fill that emptiness, respectfully remind the mind that the empty feeling has nothing to do with your tummy being empty. To fill your tummy to the point of making you fat will most probably make you end up even more empty because you will become ashamed of your size and stop going out. When that part is listening, paying attention, wanting to help, and is willing to negotiate, let it lift your 'Yes' finger. When the finger lifts, thank it for trying to help but respectfully remind it that the way it is helping you has now become a problem. You would be much more able to fill that empty feeling in life, if you were smart and fit and not over-weight. So ask it if it would help you to cope with that feeling by helping you to reduce your intake of food so that you become smarter, more fit, and a normal weight. Thank it when it agrees.

EXERCISE 7.
If you get a positive answer to question 6 and you don't have an efficient switch off feeling to eating when you have had a reasonable sized meal, respectfully remind the part of your mind that it is trying to help you cope with any of the problems above by making it easy to eat more without feeling full. Ask it to change by letting you become aware of the amount of food you have eaten at any meal. Respectfully remind it that over eating has now become a problem and you would rather not eat so much. Ask it to help you to stop over eating from now.

EXERCISE 8.
If you regularly eat everything on your plate just because it's there, and you have been taught to clean your plate or feel guilty you need to relearn that behaviour. The best way to do that is to tell your mind that it is much better, and healthier for you to throw away any unwanted food than eat it and become fat. To remind you of this, always leave at least one mouthful on your plate and throw it away, telling yourself that you don't want it, until you can do that easily, and without any feelings of guilt. When you have no guilt feeling as a reaction to throwing away food, ask your mind to

continue to help you to only eat that which you want.

EXERCISE 9.
If you are eating to win, or to feel that you are a good person, find the part of your mind that is making you do this and respectfully remind it that now that you have become over-weight you can feel much better if you don't over-eat, and will win when you reach your target weight.

EXERCISE 10.
If you have learned to reward yourself with sweets, or food, remind your mind that now you have a weight problem the reward will be getting slimmer. You will feel much healthier when you have lost some weight and that will be a reward in itself.

EXERCISE 11.
If you are eating because you feel weak, or cold, tell your mind that a good balanced diet will make you a lot stronger when you are not having to carry all that excess weight about, and you can easily put more clothes on if you feel cold.

EXERCISE 12.
If you respect something in your mother or father you can be like them without being fat like them. Tell your mind while in a hypnotic state that you can be even better than either of your parent by being like them, but without their handicap of being over-weight.

EXERCISE 13.
If you feel hungry all the time, unless you are eating, tell your mind in a hypnotic state that you would really like to only feel hungry when your blood sugar is getting low.

   If there are other concepts making you over-eat then reframe those concepts as in the above exercises. If you get a 'No' answer to all the thirteen questions on pages 14-15, and you are not losing weight, your ideo-motor finger is lying, otherwise you would have no difficulty in dieting and being a normal weight. If it needs to lie there must be a very strong reason for over-eating and that reason will need to be analysed before weight loss will be easy.

All the above exercises are intended to help you to not over-eat, and are essential if you want to keep your weight down when you have reached your target, and will also assist in losing weight. If a weight gain is achieved you must ask all the ideo-motor questions again and reframe any with a positive answer over again. If, however, you want to lose weight you must eat less than you need, and use up some of your body fat in order to reduce weight. The following exercises are intended to help you do that when you choose a reducing diet.

EXERCISE 14.
In a hypnotic state tell yourself to eat slowly and enjoy every mouthful so that you need fewer mouthfuls to get sufficient enjoyment.

EXERCISE 15.
'Spiegel's Split Screen'. Having done exercise 1. and reached the stage when you feel as if the mind is floating, project an image of a screen divided down the middle onto the far side of the room. If you can see the screen so much the better but if you can't just think about it. You cannot think about anything without creating an image. The image may be visual or conceptual, but either way you create an image. When you have the image of the screen, place on one side of the screen an image of yourself eating to excess and indulging in lots of fattening things. Notice in that image, yourself getting fatter and fatter in the places which you least like. On the other side of the screen have an image of yourself eating only the diet you have chosen, and notice how you become much more the shape you wish to be. Now choose which 'You' you want to be, and tell your mind. Bring back from the screen the 'You' you want, leaving the 'You' you don't want on the other side of the room. Imagine what it would be like, enjoying being that 'You' and integrate that feeling throughout your mind. When you can feel how enjoyable it will be, being much slimmer, and sticking to an

enjoyable diet, just open your eyes and be that 'You'.

Always remember if you have to do something, or want to do it, it is much easier if you find a way of enjoying it. Find a way of enjoying the new 'You', slimmer, healthier, and eating much less than when you were overweight. See how much more energy you will have, to do all the things you want. Notice how much more concentration you have, to do the things you want, because you are not nearly so tired as you used to be when you were so overweight. Remember when you were a stone overweight it is like carrying a stone of potatoes round with you every where you go. Notice how much more attractive you can be to the opposite sex when you are not so fat. Notice how many more options you have being normal size. See how much easier it is to get good looking clothes to fit you when you are not obese. Make sure you are going to enjoy eating the diet foods, because it is much easier to eat what you enjoy so why not programme yourself to enjoy the diet. Don't tell yourself, or anyone else, that you hate any diet food you intend to eat. You did a good job programming yourself to eat to excess so do just as good a job on dieting.

EXERCISE 16.
'Spiegel's respect for body'. When you are in a hypnotic state tell yourself that excess, or fattening foods are very bad for your body and will destroy it. Your body is your most prized and valuable possession. It is much more valuable to you than your home, or your car, or any of your jewellery, or any of your possessions. All of those things can be replaced, but your body can't. Without a body you can have none of those things. From now on, and for the rest of your life you will give your body the respect and concern it deserves. Open your eyes and give it that respect by not over-eating.

EXERCISE 17.
In order to have an accurate body image of yourself take photographs of yourself in revealing clothes and keep looking at them until you know how you look, then tell yourself how you want to look, when you are in a hypnotic

state.

Weigh yourself at least twice a week, preferably at the same time and in the same state of dress each time. Plan on losing about three to four pounds each week until your target weight is reached. Don't try to guess your weight by the feel of your clothes. Know what a sensible weight for you should be, taking into account your build etc. Don't try on any account to go well below your target weight. Eat more if you find yourself going too low. Try and find a sensible way to keep stable at your target when you reach that level.

Do at least one of the above exercises for no more that two to three minutes every two to three hours of your waking day, until you have obtained your target, and when your target is reached do the exercises over again if ever your weight becomes unstable. If you find one exercise doesn't work then do something else

EXERCISE 18.
Using ideo-motor finger questioning as described on page 21, ask the unconscious mind if it feels more mature or adult or even 'macho' smoking cigarettes? If yes, reframe that by showing the unconscious mind that it is much more mature, adult and even more macho to rely on oneself instead of a stick of dried up leaves which one sets alight to 'KID' oneself. Tell yourself it is not mature or 'macho' to con yourself.

EXERCISE 19.
If the ideo-motor finger rises to the question, 'does cigarette smoking make you more relaxed, less tense, or soothe your nerves', then you must reframe that book in the library of the unconscious by explaining that smoking is irritating to the extent of causing serious health risks and there are much better ways of feeling relaxed than conning oneself. Tell yourself smoking is irritating, not relaxing.

EXERCISE 20.
If smoking helps you to concentrate you must reframe that by telling yourself that smoking burns the oxygen out of the air that you breathe so that your brain is starved of oxygen and is

less efficient, so smoking makes concentration worse, not better.

EXERCISE 21.
If smoking helps you to belong, reframe that by telling yourself that there are more people now who don't smoke, so smoking is anti-social and smelly and irritating to non-smokers and as you are now a non-smoker you are letting yourself down and giving up what you want to be by smoking, so you don't want to smoke.

EXERCISE 22.
[SPIEGEL'S BODY IMAGE.] Tell yourself when you are in a state of hypnosis that your body is your most valuable and precious possession. Cigarette smoke is poison to your body. You are going to give your body the consideration and concern it deserves. Your body is much more valuable to you than your home or car. If you were going to manure your roses you wouldn't put the manure on your best carpet or on the back seat of your car, yet your body is much more valuable to you than your carpet or back seat of your car. Cigarette smoke is more damaging to your body than manure is to your home, so you will give as much if not more respect to your body as you can't change your body, you can change your car, or carpet.

EXERCISE 23.
[SPIEGEL'S SPLIT SCREEN] While you are in a relaxed state of hypnosis and you feel your mind floating, create an image of a screen on the other side of the room divided down the middle. On one side of the screen have an image of yourself smoking and doing all sorts of damage to your body by so doing. On the other side of the screen have an image of yourself being a non-smoker, giving your body the consideration and concern it deserves, and choose and tell your mind which 'You' you want to be. Bring back from the screen the 'You' you want to be, leaving the 'You' you don't want on the other side of the room. Integrate the 'You' you want by feeling how it would be to be a non-smoker. Then just

open your eyes and be a non-smoker.

EXERCISE 24.
For patients who have young children who don't like you
smoking. Place a picture of your children into the packet of
cigarettes that you are currently carrying where it will be seen
as soon as you open the packet. When you see the picture of
your children [child] ask yourself if you want to set your
children an example they might not be able to resist, and
result in you being responsible for them getting cancer. Do
you need a cigarette more than the example you could set
your children? Ask the patient if they find themselves getting
in some ways more like their parents in spite of themselves.
Nearly everyone does find in some way they get more like
their parents even in those ways they don't admire in their
parents.

I was asked to help a man who had a young daughter who
hated his smoking. His wife had died of lung cancer due to
smoking, so naturally his fifteen-year-old daughter didn't
want to lose him too. He had tried to give up unsuccessfully
so I asked him to put a photograph of his daughter in his
packet of cigarettes and he never smoked another cigarette.

Do at least one of the above exercises every two to three
hours of your waking day, spending no more than two
minutes on the exercise until you have no desire to con
yourself any more about smoking, and you are happy to be a
non-smoker. If someone should offer you a cigarette say 'no
thank you I don't smoke'. Don't say 'I have given it up'. If
you say 'I have given it up', you may well cause some guilt
feelings in the person offering you the cigarette as they most
probably have at some time thought they should give it up,
and been unsuccessful. They may well try to relieve their
own guilt by trying to persuade you to smoke. It is hard
enough, without smoking to relieve someone elses guilt. If
you say 'I don't smoke', most people will accept that without
feeling guilty.

Don't be tempted to substitute smoking with another form
of oral gratification. Over-eating is the most common way
people try to overcome smoking and then they have to start

to smoke to lose weight. This substitute is just another way we have for cheating on ourselves. I once read in a hypnotic journal a case history where the hypnotist was recommending to the patient that they should reward themselves for not smoking by having a box of chocolates. I wondered if they returned for treatment for smoking and over-weight? It is always better to suggest at sometime in the hypnotic treatment that the patient will not be tempted to over eat as a substitute.

Remember it is almost impossible to cut down on smoking, it is an 'all-or-nothing' thing. Don't be tempted in an 'anchor situation' to just have one cigarette, it won't end there. Every time you resist an 'anchor situation' without smoking, the anchor will get weaker. It may be necessary to help someone to cope with 'anchor situations' by taking them through the situation in hypnotic dream or enactment and seeing themselves still being a non—smoker. If all or any of the above exercises don't work, then it will probably be necessary to find out exactly why the patient needs to smoke. If one thing doesn't work in hypnosis then do something else, don't just keep on doing the same old thing hoping that eventually it may work.

I once was asked to help a man to be a non-smoker who managed to override all attempts to help him. In the end he admitted he didn't really want to stop smoking he really wanted to see if he could trust me to help him with another much more personal and private problem. I did help him with that problem and he is much happier but still smokes. You have no right to tell people what they should do unless they ask for help. This presents the main difficulty in treating children smokers, most of them don't want to stop. They refuse to admit they are addicted and until they do there is very little anyone can do. Most of them even refuse to talk about smoking, and if you try to get them to talk, they become very defensive, which only goes to show how much their unconscious mind really needs the dynamic processes discussed in this chapter connected with the habit of smoking. Most parents also seem to refuse to take any responsibility for their childrens' behaviour and pass the buck onto the schools. [See next chapter on alcohol and drug taking.]

EXERCISE 25.
Treatment of Alcoholism by N.L.P. Reframing.
Find out which situations make you drink. *[What are the 'Anchor' situations which make you want to drink?]* When you know all the situations in which you would normally want to drink then enter the hypnotic state as in Exercise 1. Start with the first situation and create an image of yourself in that situation and be very positive in your mind that drinking will not help, but only make it worse and compound your difficulties. Ask your mind to find another way of helping you to cope with that situation without making you want to drink. Repeat this exercise with all the situations in which you normally would resort to drink and ask your mind to find other ways of helping you.

Having done this, set up an ideo-motor finger response as in Exercise 2. and ask the part of your mind that makes you drink, when it is listening, paying attention, wanting to help you and is willing to negotiate, to lift your 'Yes' finger high in the air. When your finger lifts, ask it if it willing to let you know what secondary gain is achieved by drinking. [i.e. confidence, relaxation, relief of any form of pain,(physical or psychological), camaraderie, relief from guilt, etc.] If it is willing, let it lift your 'Yes' finger. If it is not willing to let you know what the secondary gain is, let it lift your 'No' finger.

If your 'Yes' finger lifts ask it to let your mind know now what the secondary gain is. If your 'No' finger lifts then just go on to the next part without knowing. It is more helpful if you know what the gain is consciously, but if your mind is unwilling to let you know now it is generally due to a poor ego image *[a low opinion of your self that may be made even worse if you have to know consciously what the secondary gain is, you receive from drinking.]* Your unconscious mind knows what the gain is otherwise it couldn't produce that gain unconsciously for you. You should on no account try to force your mind to reveal anything it feels uncomfortable about. You may find as you get stronger your mind will willingly disclose the gain at a later time. In either case go on to the next part of this exercise described below.

Now find another part of your mind that can help you achieve the same secondary gain, without having to resort to drink. When you have found another part that will help you achieve the same gain without producing the damage that alcohol does, ask it to get together with the part that makes you drink, and persuade the part that makes you drink to help you in this new and better way. Ask both parts if they will produce the secondary gain in this new and better way in all the situations that in the past would have made you resort to drink. When they feel confident that they will now help you in this better way let them both lift your 'Yes' finger. You don't have to know consciously what this better way is for it to work.

A person will always make the best choice available to him or her in any situation. Before this reframing your mind didn't realise it had a choice. You have just shown it there are better ways of coping. If you offer your mind better choices than drinking to get all the positive secondary gains of alcohol, your mind will make the better selections, and you can stop having to drink.

It is very possible that the above exercise will have to be done with a therapist for the first few times as it may be difficult to remember all of the exercise on your own, especially when your eyes are shut, and a therapist can suit the treatment to your individual needs and 'Anchor' situations. Remember every time you resist an 'Anchor' situation the 'Anchor' becomes weaker.

This exercise, and the following ones can all be used for any addiction. Just substitute, for alcohol, which ever drug you are addicted to, in any of these exercises.

EXERCISE 26.
[SPIEGEL'S SPLIT SCREEN.] While you are in a relaxed state of hypnosis and feel your mind floating, create an image of a screen on the other side of the room, divided down the middle. On one side of the screen have an image of yourself drinking and doing all sorts of damage to your body and

mind by being drunk, and being obnoxious as a result of being intoxicated. On the other side of the screen have an image of yourself not drinking at all, giving your body and mind and friends the consideration and concern they deserve. See how much clearer you can think and behave, and how much you prefer this you. Tell your mind which 'You' you want to be, and bring back from the screen the 'You' you want to be, leaving the 'You' you don't want on the other side of the room. Integrate the 'You' you want by feeling how it is, to not drink, then open your eyes and don't drink.

For treatment of other drug addictions, substitute the other drug for alcohol

EXERCISE 27.
[SPIEGEL'S BODY IMAGE.] Tell yourself when you are in a state of hypnosis that your body and mind are your most valuable and precious possessions. Alcohol [or other drug] is poison to your body and mind. You are going to give your body and mind the consideration and concern it deserves. Open your eyes and give your body and mind that consideration.

Do these last two exercises every two to three hours for two minutes at a time during your waking hours, until you no longer want to drink alcohol, [or take the drug], and repeat if ever your desire to drink, [or take the drug] returns

EXERCISE 28.
Put yourself into a hypnotic state by turning your eyes up to look at your eyebrows, keeping your eyes turned up close your lids and at the same time 'let go'. Now turn your mind inwards to look at your mind and tell yourself the following five reasons for not biting your nails, one for each finger and thumb.

1. A little reason for a little finger. I will not bite my little finger because I'm hungry or tense because there is no food value in nails. In any case I spit the nail out so I don't need to get satisfaction by biting the nail so I won't.

2. Nails don't taste nice. They are covered with germs and bacteria that I pick up from all the surfaces that I touch so I won't bite my nails and I will be much healthier because I won't be putting germs and bacteria into my mouth.

3. When I was small I used to put my fingers into my mouth to comfort me, but grown ups don't do that. I will show myself and the world that I'm grown up, and have much better ways of reducing stress than biting my nails. In any case biting my nails makes me tense, afterwards, so I won't bite them any more.

4. Every time I put my hand out to shake someone by the hand I will feel proud of my hands, not ashamed because my nails will look good and manicured because I no longer bite my nails. I will never have to hide my hands again because I can be proud of them.

5. The last and big reason for not biting my nails. My hands are a part of my whole body and self. As I see my nails growing good and strong I will begin to like them like that, and as I do I will succeed in liking myself much more and feel much more mature and confident in myself.

I have just given myself five good reasons for not biting my nails so everytime my hands begin to move to my mouth to bite my nails I will become very aware that I don't do that anymore. Fairly quickly when both my conscious and unconscious mind know that, I will relegate that instruction to my unconscious and I will never even think of biting my nails again.

Now just open your eyes and enjoy your nails, looking good.

Do this exercise every two hours for two minutes at a time until you never think of biting your nails.

Milton Erickson describes another exercise for stopping biting your nails shown below in exercise 29.

EXERCISE 29.
In the hypnotic state tell your mind that you obviously get a relief of tension or something from biting your nails, but as you have five fingers on each hand you could leave one

finger on each hand to grow big and long. Open your eyes and leave that finger to grow.

When that finger is beautifully manicured look and see how much more beautiful that one looks in comparison to the other four.

Again in the hypnotic state tell yourself that perhaps you could leave another finger to grow beautiful.

When you have two beautiful fingers tell yourself to have three, then four. When you have four beautiful fingers tell yourself it's a pity to spoil your hands with one finger so let them all grow beautiful.

EXERCISE 30.
Speigels' Split Screen.
In the hypnotic state create an image of yourself, on one side of a screen, with bitten fingernails, hiding your hands and looking ashamed and angry with yourself for being so immature. On the other side of the screen have an image of yourself with beautifully manicured nails, feeling pleased, proud and mature. Tell your mind which 'You' you want to be, and bring that 'You' back from the screen, leaving the 'You' you don't want on the other side of the room. Open your eyes and be that 'You'.

Do this exercise every two hours for two minutes at a time until your nails are grown, and beautiful.

EXERCISE 31.
Speigels' Split Screen.
In a hypnotic state make an image on one side of a screen of yourself sucking your thumb. See how childish you look, and because you are acting childishly see how unhappy you really are. See how sucking your thumb is even making your life worse because no one takes you seriously.

On the other side of the screen see yourself coping with life in a much more mature way without sucking your thumb. See how much more seriously other people take you now that you don't just behave childishly. See how much happier you are, now that you are getting wiser every day. Now chose which 'You' you want to be, and tell your mind. Bring back from the screen the 'You' you want and open your eyes and be that 'You'

EXERCISE 32.
Geoff Graham's Scrap Book technique for confidence.

In the Hypnotic state imagine a beautiful book on your knee with your name on the front. On the first page picture yourself sitting in the chair that you are actually sitting in, with your eyes closed, in a deep hypnotic state. To anyone else looking at that picture, they may think you are asleep, but you know you are not asleep. You know your mind is so attentive to whatever you tell it, that you will feel the emotions connected with what you are telling it, just as if the thing you are telling yourself were happening to you now. Now look at that picture and feel how comfortable you are now.

Now look at how well you have learned to go into the hypnotic state, and feel that now. Feel how successful you are at entering the hypnotic state, and hang on to that success. Use that feeling of success to feel the success you are at being a very good solicitor's secretary. Picture that in your scrap book. [In this place put anything you do well, no matter how small a thing that may be, and feel how good it is to do something well.] Hold on to that good feeling, and imagine how good it would be to be wide awake with that good feeling.

Before you open your eyes look at another picture in your scrap book of a time when you felt marvellously relaxed and happy. Hold on to that relaxed feeling, hold on to that happy feeling. Now imagine how good it would be to be wide awake with that relaxed, happy and successful feeling. Open your eyes and be wide awake with that relaxed, happy, and successful feeling and do whatever you are doing, with those good feelings. When you do, you will probably do, whatever you are doing much better, with those good feelings. Put those things you do better in your scrap book the next time you look at it, and as your scrap book grows thicker and thicker with things you do well you can't help becoming more confident in everything that you are doing. [This is taking the well accepted concept of free floating anxiety, and working it in reverse by taking a good event and using the positive emotion from that to feel good now. With free floating anxiety you are taking a negative event and using the bad emotion to feel bad now.]

Repeat looking at your mental scrap book for two minutes at a time, every two hours, until you feel very well, and repeat if you lose that good feeling.

EXERCISE 33.
Calvert Stein's clenched fist for tension reduction.

When you are in a hypnotic state think about something really good and strong, and imagine that you could hold that really good and strong thing in your dominant hand. Make a fist in your dominant hand and squeeze that good and strong thing until you feel as if the strength and goodness was going into your hand and up your arm and into your body. Hold on to that feeling.

Now think about any tension you can feel in your body and realize how negative that tension is. Make a fist in your non-dominant hand and imagine as you grip your non-dominant hand that all the tension is being drawn down into your non-dominant fist. Feel that tension being drawn down into your non-dominant fist and when it is all in your fist, hold on tight to it and don't let it back into your body.

While you are holding, tightly, all the negative tension in your body in your non-dominant fist, think about that really good and strong thing again in your dominant fist. Squeeze up your dominant fist and feel all that good strength moving up your dominant arm into your body, across your shoulders and down your non-dominant arm to your clenched fist. When all that good strong feeling reaches your non-dominant fist just open your non-dominant hand and let all the negative tension be pushed out by that good strong feeling. When all the negative tension has been pushed out of your fist by your good strong feeling onto the floor just open your dominant hand and feel relaxed, good and strong all over. Remember your dominant hand is always stronger than your non-dominant hand.

Repeat this exercise for two minutes at a time three or four times a day until you feel good and strong all the time and repeat if the feeling leaves you.

EXERCISE 34.
In the Hypnotic state contact that part of your mind that makes you gag on food. [You can substitute here, for gagging, any other behaviour you may want to rid yourself of.] Thank that part of your mind for trying to help you by making you gag. Then respectfully remind it that unfortunately the way it is trying to help you, by making you gag, has become the problem. While that part is listening, paying attention and wanting to help you, contact another part of your mind that weighs up all the pro's and con's of everything you do. Thank that part for helping you and ask both parts to get together in your unconscious mind, to debate and discuss ways that the first part could continue to help you without having to make you gag.

When they have discussed and agreed on a few ways in which the first part could help you, without having to make you gag, thank them both. Ask the first part to try some of these new ways of helping you until you find a better way of behaving. You will not be consciously aware of how they are going to help you because you asked them, deliberately, to discuss and debate the ways in your unconscious mind. This is done this way because if you know how the part is going to help you, you may try too hard to make it work which may spoil it and stop it from working. Sometimes the harder you try to do something the more impossible it becomes to do it. If you don't know, consciously, you will just do it, and may be pleasantly surprised. If you are not, repeat the exercise until you are.

EXERCISE 35.
Speigel's split screen.
In the hypnotic state create an image of a screen, divided down the middle, on the other side of the room. On one side of the screen, create an image of yourself gagging on your food, and always being aware and focusing your attention on

the pain in your back.

On the other side of the screen create an image of yourself eating and enjoying all your food. Also see yourself being much more interested in what you are doing and what is going on around you so that you hardly notice your back.

Tell your mind which 'You' you want to be, and bring back from the screen the 'You' you want to be, leaving the 'You' you don't want on the other side of the room. Integrate the 'You' you want by feeling what it would be like to be that 'You' and open your eyes and be that 'You'.

EXERCISE 36.
Changing new for old for woman patients.

I have emphasised the important parts in the metaphor in bold print.

Having got my patient comfortably seated with her shoes off and both of her feet flat on the ground I ask her to 'just close your eyes.' Then I say the following to her.

'I would like you for a moment to think about your eyes. They are your windows on to the world. You can send messages out from them. You can show love, hate, hunger, anger, fear, guilt, and all your emotions just by looking in different ways. At the same time your eyes can take messages in. When a light beam falls on to your eye the lens at the front of your eye concentrates the beam on to small cells, in the shape of rods and cones, at the back of your eye. These cells as a result of the light being concentrated on them produce certain chemicals. Those chemicals excite the nerve at the back of your eye and create an electrical impulse to pass back along the nerve through the hole in the back of your eyeball into the brain. And still you haven't seen anything. The nerve in the brain then crosses over to the other side of the brain and excites more nerves. And still you haven't seen anything All this would happen if you were asleep and someone gently opened your eyelid and looked into your eye. If you didn't wake up you wouldn't see anything.

The nerves that have now been excited send an impulse to the visual centre in your brain to alert and wake up that part of your brain and at last you see something. At the same time other nerves send impulses to your memory centre to help you to identify what ever you are now seeing. Your memory centre has millions of little circuits with all sorts of memories.

There was an interesting programme on the television sometime ago about a girl who was blind and the eye surgeons decided if they did an operation on her eyes she may be able to see. They did the operation and when the bandages were removed, much to everyones delight, she could see. They did some very interesting experiments while the girl was sitting at a table. They placed a cup on the table and asked her if she knew what it was. She didn't know what it was until they pushed it towards her and asked her to pick it up. When her hands touched it she laughed and said it's a cup. She had no visual memory of a cup because she had never seen a cup before, but she had a tactile memory of a cup because she had drunk out of a cup many times and touched a cup many times. As soon as she touched it she recognised it as a cup. **She had to learn all over again what everything looked like before she could visually identify what everything was.**

All our memories are stored in little compartments in our brain. Those compartments could be like your bedroom with wardrobes and a chest of drawers and a dressing table and perhaps a bookshelf for your books. You have specific places to keep all your special things. Sometimes if your things have just been washed, or you have just been looking at them, and you haven't yet had time to put them away you may need your bedroom, because guests are coming to visit you, and you want to put your guests coats on your bed while they are with you. You may just push your things into the wardrobe to make the room look tidy for the time being, but after they have gone **you will have to go back and tidy up properly, and put all your things in their proper place**.

One day you may be walking down the high street and while you are passing a little dress shop, there in the window on a model is the most beautiful dress, just your colour and style. You can't believe your luck because it has been reduced from a ridiculous price to a real bargain. You can't resist going in and asking the sales girl if you can try it on. She is pleased to help you and shows you to a changing room and brings the dress. You quickly take off the dress you are wearing and put on the new one and you turn to look at it in the mirror. When you see it a thrill goes right through you. **It fits you perfectly. It does something for you, shows off all your best qualities. It's just your colour.** [When this exercise is over it is often useful to ask what colour the dress was. The colour may give a clue to what is in the patients unconscious mind at the time.] **It seems to bring out your best personality and makes you feel very confident.** You decide to have it, so you take it off and put on the dress you came in with. Taking the new dress to the sales girl you say you will take it, so she wraps it up for you and you pay the money and go out of the shop.

Outside you can't really believe everything you thought inside the shop so you hurry home and rush up to your bedroom. There, you pull off the wrapping and **examine the dress again**. It still looks just as good and all the stitching is perfect and there are no marks on it. Quickly you once again take off your dress and try on the new one. It looks even better, **fits you even better than you dared think. You feel a million dollars in it. You are very pleased with yourself**.

You decide you don't want to wear it right now, but will keep it for a special occasion, so you take it carefully off and once again put your old one back on. You go with it to your wardrobe to hang it up but when you open your wardrobe door you find that all the hangers are in use. You don't have a spare one to hang your beautiful new dress on so you have to look through all your dresses until you find an old one. **One that doesn't fit any more, that is worn, or out of fashion. One that does nothing for you, or that you have ceased to like. One that doesn't suit your new personality.** When you find one that is no use to you anymore you take it out and place your new one on that hanger and put it carefully in your wardrobe and close the door. **You feel good, even just knowing it is there when you want it.** You take the old one and send it off to Oxfam, or cut it up for dusters, or just put it in the dustbin.

You feel very pleased with yourself. **It's always necessary,** once in a while, to look through your old things and have a good clean out. You throw away the old useless things, which you have accumulated over the years, discarding those which do nothing for you anymore. Your mind is just like that.'

To order a copy for yourself or a friend or patient by mail order sent to—

REAL OPTIONS PRESS,
Dunsopp House
Lucy Street
Blaydon upon Tyne.
NE21 5PU
U.K.

....Cut here

Book by the same Author
With self help exercises to help a person mature and become responsible for themselves and therefore have many more options in their lives.

Please send........ Copies of 'HOW TO BECOME THE PARENT YOU NEVER HAD' by GEOFF GRAHAM ISBN 0 9511951 0 7 to

Name..

Address..

....

....

.... Post Code...........

I enclose £6.95 + £1.05 [post and package] for each book U.K. market or $10 + $6 [post and package] for U.S.A. market.

....

'IT'S A BIT OF A MOUTHFUL' by GEOFF GRAHAM
ISBN 0 9511951 1 5

With self help exercises for Obesity, Smoking, Alcoholism, Oral Sex, Anorexia Nervosa, Nail Biting, Thumb Sucking, Dental Phobia and other Dental problems.

Please send........copies of 'IT'S A BIT OF A MOUTHFUL' by GEOFF GRAHAM to

Name...

Address..

....

....

.... Post Code...............

I enclose £6.95 +£1.05 [post and package] for each book U.K. market or $10 +$6 [post and package] for U.S.A market.

Please send the completed order, with cheque, to 'Real Options Press, Dunsopp House, Lucy Street. Blaydon upon Tyne. NE21 5PU. U.K.

Please Print Name and Address clearly.